STRESS-FREE DISCIPLINE

2 Cor. 9:8
Judith Bonner

JUDITH DeSELM BONNER

Legacy Line Publishing
San Diego, California 92119

STRESS-FREE DISCIPLINE

ISBN: 978-0-98197-848-2

Published by:

Legacy Line Publishing
7287 Birchcreek Rd.
San Diego, CA 92119

Toll-free: 1-866-757-9953

www.legacylinepublishing.com

Strong's Exhaustive Concordance of the Bible by James Strong, Zondervan Publishing House, also used.

Printed in the United States of America.

"The primary cause of most behavior and student achievement problems in the public school system is irresponsible and/or incompetent parents...No child is more handicapped than a child whose parents don't understand and accept the responsibilities of parenthood. Poor parents destroy the lives of more children in this country than drugs, alcohol, and gangs combined."

Stanley Bippus,
Superintendent of Central
Consolidated School District,
Farmington, New Mexico,
Daily Times, September 4, 1994

The rod and reproof give wisdom, but a child left to himself brings shame to his mother.

Proverbs 29:15, NKJV

Parent's Prayer

Dear Lord, thank you.
You have redeemed us out of destruction,
Delivered us from the power of sin in our lives,
Given us your lovingkindness and mercy.

Help us, Father, to express your love to our children
In ways that teach them to honor You above all.
Help us so we do not bruise Your fruit, Lord.

Make us always aware of your desire for us,
Our duties, our hope and delight in you.
Renew our motives. Stretch us and strengthen us in You.
Expand our awareness of Your love.

Help us to commit all our resources to building Your Kingdom.
Purify our aims, ambitions, and activity.
Focus our scattered lives.
Teach us, that we may master Your lessons.
Make them second nature.

Dear Father, only You can expand our spiritual,
Mental and emotional boundaries beyond our small selves.

Help us to create, out of the confusion of our lives,
Spiritually strong teams in our church and homes.
You are the great I AM, giver of every good gift.
Thank you for the gifts we already enjoy.
The greatest of these is our children.

Amen

Dedication

This work is dedicated to my sons, Anthony and Charles Jeter, who raised me from their childhood! Their encouragement and support, prodding, critiques and inspiration have blessed me immeasurably. I also thank my parents. It was their intelligence, persistence, endurance, aid and comfort which helped me slog through the dark times and enjoy the sunshine. Thank you Mike Bonner, my husband, for your encouragement and support. Most importantly, I dedicate this, my life's work, to the glory of the LORD, my strength and Redeemer.

Acknowledgments

My deepest gratitude goes to Jo Lynne Jones and Dr. Frederic Jones, who have generously allowed foundational elements in their *Tools for Teaching* to provide some discipline guidance for my book *Stress-free Discipline.*

Gratitude is due to many who were sources of review and hands-on encouragement: Pastors Kenny Dodd, Joseph Han; Dr. William C. Reeves, Ph.D. Human Behavior; Dr. Janette Gray, Clairemont Emmanuel Baptist Church Young Married Class members and other church members; Yolanda and Dave Pearson, Julie and Gary Kirk and best of all, my husband, Mike J. Bonner.

My son, Charles Jeter, has given technical and moral support beyond any mother's reasonable expectation. Thank you, Lord, that you raised up a blessing!

Table of Contents

Parent's Prayer iv
Dedication v
Acknowledgments vii
Foreword xiii
Preface xv

Section I

Discipline Dynamics

What Must We Know and Be in Order to Create Stress-free Discipline? 21
Foundations: Recognize the Grip of Adrenalin 25
Avoid a Vicious Cycle 27
Eliminate Cultural Stresses 29
Beware of the High Cost of Permissive Parenting 31
Avoid Stress Caused by Personality Differences 32
Practice "Unnatural" Parenting 34
Find Time for Loving Relationships .37
Be Aware of Stress Cycles 39
Create Freedom with Accountability .40
Free Yourself While You Build Healthy Self-esteem in Your Children 41
Use and Know Creative, Purposeful Discipline 44
One Example – Teaching Money Management 45
Strategy: Master Truly Effective Discipline 48
Internalize the Goals of Discipline 51
Build Teamwork: Healthy Interdependence 52
Beware of Myths and Mistakes in Discipline 54
Grasp the Big Picture 56

Reinforce Goal-driven Choices 59
Understand Biblically-based Authority 62
Perfect Your Skills — Be Accountable 65
Model Assertiveness, Not Aggression 68
Maintain Your Accountability 70
Understand the Strong-willed Child 76

Section II

What You Must Know About Methods and Materials

View and Review the Expectations and Point Charts 81
Understand and Foster Maturity 88
Set Your Family Up for Success 92
Build Team Spirit 94
Set (Do Not Destroy) Boundaries with Your Body Language . . .97
Prevent Misbehavior By Moving in Close 100
Practice Moving in Techniques to Set Yourself Up for Success 101
Master Crucial Skills: Practice, Practice, Practice 102
Understand Your Child's Body Language 104
Practice Your Moving Away Technique .106
Confront Continual Misbehavior 106
Ignore All Back Talk But Take Off Points 109
Master the Follow-up Sequence 112
Think Through and Practice Your Back-up Strategy 117
Acting Out: What If It Does Not Stop? .124
Enjoy the Price of Sainthood: Impulse Control and Attention Span 127
Win the Reward: Lasting Love 128
Use These Tips 129

Section III

What Must We Do To Put Stress-free Discipline into Practice?

Establish Goals 133
Follow This System for Introducing the Charts 134
Parents' Duty and Skill List 157
Evaluate and Practice Your Teaching Methods 164
Build Self-confidence Through Excellence and Growth 176
Use Motivational Games for Reward Time 181
Success Is Biblical, Reasoned Choices .188

Section IV

Questions and Answers

Appendices

Appendix A
Personality Analysis 205

Appendix B
The Stress-busting Technique of Deep Breathing 218

Appendix C
The Importance of Acid-Alkaline Balance 221

Appendix D
About Spanking 224

Appendix E
Problem-solving Matrix 225

Appendix F
Getting the Most Work for the Least Effort Through Prioritizing227

Appendix G
Brain-builders Step By Step 230

Appendix H
Teaching Tips for Preschool Children .233

Appendix I
How Do I Know When My Child Has Mastered the Chart? 236

Appendix J
Use Music at 60 Beats Per Minute (No Words!) 238

Appendix K
Exercising Your Way Out of Your Right Brain Comfort Zone . .241

Appendix L
Exercise Your Way Out of Your Left Brain Comfort Zone 243

Appendix M
How Stress-free Discipline Looks in Practice
(rarely glitch-free) 245

Appendix N
Printable Charts 253

About the Author 267

End Notes 269

Foreword

Stress-free Discipline is an excellent guide for parents seeking positive, purposeful and creative disciplinary ideas to lead their children through all stages of childhood. Physical correction is addressed as an appropriate tool at times when used properly. The main thrust is to plan ahead and reward children for positive behavior.

> A seminar setting is an especially good way to learn how to utilize the tools found in *Stress-free Discipline*. This resource can give many pertinent ideas to parents to help them through all ages of a child's path to self-discipline and maturity.

William C. Reeves, Ph.D., Human Behavior Counselor Emeritus, Clairemont Emmanuel Church Counseling Center

Preface

"Why should I add this project to my already busy schedule? And what does this system have over another discipline system?" Have you found yourself thinking these thoughts? Let me share some points that might help you with your decision.

- Basics of this system have been tested and used in classrooms across the country.
- This system causes poor behavior to self-eliminate without parents using intimidation or violence (but spanking is allowed when appropriate).
- It rewards good behavior consistently (with free and low cost motivators).
- It gives timesaving consequences for both good and poor behavior.
- Small disturbances are consistently caught so children are discouraged from risking larger ones.
- It builds teamwork while raising the performance bar for both parents and children.
- It is flexible and can be tailored to fit your family expectations, yet the recommended expectations are sufficient without change.
- Stress relief for parents is built into this system, while gentle pressure is kept on the children to obey.
- This system grows with the children, step by step, encouraging a lifelong supportive, interdependent

relationship with parents and with each other when they are adults.

- Rewards for good behavior always carry more points (educational time spent with you) than negative points for poor choices. It is better motivation to behave well than use simple punishment.
- Rebellion, however, carries "double jeopardy," making it unattractive to children.
- Parents and children are united in finding cooperative, supportive, creative solutions to problems which both face.
- Children gradually master complex adult expectations and goals.
- Adult skills and college-level thinking skills are built in a logical sequence.
- It is a biblically-based program.
- It helps your children to become "Bereans"—Christians who question everything in the light of Scripture.
- It prevents a child's involvement in the occult.

Stress-free Discipline not only reduces stress, it builds love, teamwork, life skills and responsibility. Like any building project, discipline requires tools, skill, work and resources. This book contains all the basic tools you need for tots-to-teens discipline. You must build your own parenting skills with this book as a resource.

You will be blessed according to the effort you put into the project. Parenting or mentoring children takes all you have to give for as long as you live.

You will pay up-front: the price is your time and effort. Thoughtful discipline will take you where you want to go, and the price is worth it. Every time you feel like giving up on this project, squash that feeling before it multiplies.

➥ Winners never quit, and quitters never win!

Discipline is much more than punishment. It includes consistent consequences, realistic expectations, and progressive benchmarks. Another aspect of discipline is training that corrects, molds or perfects mental faculties or moral character; it is also a system of rules regarding conduct. Discipline is much more than punishment! This book is a sequential program which covers all of the above.

You will create your own expectations using my suggestions as your starting point.

Benchmarks (Point Charts) are your measure of success. They must stay as I designed them. Your children are rewarded in time spent with you in educational activities. This includes training in sports, social graces, ministry, and other life skills.

➥ Your reward is their cooperation and teamwork which will save you time, work and stress. The result is a happier, well-balanced family team.

Teaching resources in this book are extensive. You can build college-level thinking skills step by step with my activities. Both you and your children will benefit with enriched thought-life built into *Stress-free Discipline*. Enrichment is a bonus. Right thinking, the basics, prevents brutal life tragedy. This book provides both frosting and cake; it builds enrichment with the basics.

Your greatest discipline resource is an essential "love bank." Punishment is the back-up consequence which is most costly—making serious withdrawals from your child's love bank. Many other effective discipline tools given here make the need for punishment—especially spankings, rare. Those tools make deposits in the love bank.

This book explores and celebrates the differences in personality and thinking styles which can make or break your discipline. It provides tools for you to better understand and love each other, turning your stresses into stretches into sainthood.

Basics of this system have been tested and used in classrooms with all kinds of able and disadvantaged children. It stops bad behavior and starts good behavior.

Realistic, skillful, thoughtful discipline prevents involvement in the occult, family dysfunction, and young victims of predators.

➥ Most importantly, this system builds your family team into Bereans: Christians who examine everything in the light of Scripture. May our Lord grant you increase of joy, peace and power in the Holy Spirit.

Section I

Discipline Dynamics

What Must We Know and Be in Order to Create Stress-free Discipline?

Have you noticed how the children get into trouble the instant you turn your back? Does your nine-year-old walk out when you tell him to stay in? Can your two-year-old pull your strings for an hour before she finally goes to bed? Did you know when you had two children that they would be four times as much trouble as one?

Stress-free Discipline is a system designed to achieve good parenting without negatively-expressed emotion. One hour of planning and carrying out this method will save you between four and twelve hours of nagging, debate and frustration with your child. Hold this thought.

Stress results from dwelling in the right brain (the feelings area) without balancing with left brain thinking. Eighty percent of women are right brain processors. That means most women will feel most comfortable with emotions, symbols, music, art, analogies, generalities, "the big picture," etc. Left brain territory (the logical, rational, linear, time-ordered, sequential, linear part) is not their comfort zone, but discomfort need not equal distress.[1] It is merely a place for whole-brain practice in order to grow comfortable.[2]

Men, you are not exempt. Twenty percent of you are pushover parents. Discipline stresses you too.

Further, our hormones, old "tapes," and feelings play ping-pong with our brains, causing us stress. We are all human. Take note: balance of left and right brain thinking puts us into a joyous place of God's grace. "God has not given us a spirit of fear, but of power, of love, and of a sound mind" (2 Timothy 1:7, KJV).

Sound mind means practice, practice, practice until we use all of our brain, not just the easy comfort zone. We "have the mind of Christ" (1 Corinthians 2:16b). Christ is not a half-wit! We only have to exercise balanced thinking. The Appendix has exercises to balance your habitual thinking style. What we call stress is God's way of stretching us!

Stress, then, is caused by failure to practice spiritual discipline. When feelings control our behavior, we fall into Satan's snares every time. Feelings must not be our CEO—our control center. The right role for feelings is as motivators when we have made thoughtful choices. Emotion helps us remember things longer and carry through on our decisions. Ideally, thoughts control feelings. God designed us that way. Body chemistry, subconscious anger, and depression, etc. are all controlled by thoughts. God's Word and prayer control thoughts. These truths shall set you free.

Positive and negative stress (eustress and distress) both cause physical reactions. Excess or chronic stress can cause chronic fatigue, headaches, poor digestion or appetite, memory loss, high blood pressure, shallow breathing, anxiety and depression. It also contributes to illness of more serious kinds, including heart disease, back problems and cancer.

Some people handle stress well; others do poorly.

- ➥ Negative stress to one personality is motivational, positive stress to another. For example, women are stressed out when they feel lonely or unloved.

Most men do not worry about feeling lonely or unloved. That only means they are following the coach's directions: "Get in front and don't look back!" Men are stressed when they feel disrespected and inadequate (see Ephesians 5:22-32). Women do not care about feeling inadequate: they stop to ask directions! All stress causes wear and tear on your body.

Stress is any reaction that upsets our body's balance. Decide now if you want to control stress or let it control you. Do you hate change? Is fast fun or comfort your goal in life regardless of long-term consequences? Are you a lazy, magical thinker, avoiding mental challenge?

If you want comfort at any price, drop this book like a hot rock. It's up to you.

If you are willing to make changes, list some of your stressors here. Remember, if you do not control stresses, they will control you (examples might be noise, ignorance, disease, pain, extremes of temperature, new job, new baby, wedding, funeral, medications, worry, lack of sleep, alcohol, personality differences, smoking):

____

____

____

____

Read over the above stressors, highlighting those you can learn to control, and setting aside those you cannot control. When you feel yourself uptight because of stressors you cannot control, remember to give them to God in prayer. You do your best, and He does the rest. He promised to give you peace, and He said, "Let peace reign in your heart."[3] He gives you the peace, but if you do not accept it, you do not have any. Keep focused on the answer, and the problems will be less disturbing. You are the one who allows peace to rule over your feelings.

Some of your stresses are self-inflicted wounds. This book explores family stresses caused by different personality and thinking styles. These stresses are God-designed challenges to stretch us into sainthood. We need to grow rather than growl at each other!

This book is a love "tool kit" which helps you understand intimate stress. Understanding not only reduces stress, it builds love. Discipline and strong marriages are both based on an essential "love bank." Love is the bond that keeps your family team running in the race set before you.

➥ Why is it important to accept, honor and celebrate different personality and thinking styles in your family?

- ➥ When we understand another's stressors, we can relieve them, enriching our love bond.
- ➥ In the process we balance our own thinking.
- ➥ Enhanced love is necessary for discipline and a lasting marriage.
- ➥ God calls us to strengthen each other.

Stress-free Discipline lightens your parenting burden because it minimizes the words exchanged while keeping pressure on the child to obey. Because there is less negative interaction, you and your child are freed to build a lasting love. (Do not worry about pressuring your child to obey. This stress will be small compared to the power struggles that normally distress both of you.)

Parents divorce over three basic issues: child rearing, finance and sex. Notice that these sources of conflict fall under the same three categories that separate us from God: lust of the eyes (misspent money), lust of the flesh (sexual problems), and pride (misbehavior of children).[4] You can minimize one of these sources of marital stress via *Stress-free Discipline.*

Ask yourself: Is a love relationship with my child important enough for me to spend the time it takes to grasp these tools and practice using them? Love is spelled "T-I-M-E." You choose how it is spent.

This system avoids what psychology professor David Miklowitz of the University of Colorado calls the "three volley." First, there is misbehavior, followed by a command, then backtalk. The family fight (with nagging and bad feelings) is on. Further, *Stress-free Discipline* is designed to eliminate the harm that can be caused by tough love, a good basic principle which can make kids who can't control their behavior feel worse about themselves.[5] Data shows that our methodology achieves better results than traditional behavior modification.

Have you noticed how the act of disciplining your child often plays ping-pong with your brain? *Stress-free Discipline* gives you a clear head to impose real-world consequences for your child's misbehavior.[6]

- *Stress-free Discipline* prevents the vicious loop of angry brainstem fight-or-flight discipline. Remember, it lightens the burden of discipline and confrontation because it minimizes the words exchanged while keeping pressure on the child to obey.

Foundations: Recognize the Grip of Adrenalin

What usually happens? The child's misbehavior triggers adrenalin in the parent, pushing the parent's thought process into the (primitive) brain stem: fight or flight behavior. Unfortunately, neither fighting nor escaping from the problem will prevent our child from repeating wrong behavior. Moreover, once we're in the brain stem, we stay in fight or flight mode for 28 minutes until the adrenalin wears off. During that time, we cannot access the skill-filled area in the front of the brain stem.[7]

Mothers under stress have two more choices of stress relief behavior: They may nurture their children and/or talk out their troubles. While nurture and connection with friends releases stress in women, it does not maintain discipline. For that matter, it does not build stronger marriages if the feedback is wrong. Pity parties do not work, and it is easier to destroy than to build your family.

Mothers can avoid some stress by getting enough sleep, eating right, and getting exercise. However, if mother's sleep is disturbed by reruns of family battles, this adds to her stress. Adrenalin kicks in for 28 minutes every time she thinks about an incident.

Practice the right timing. Recognize that nurturing your child needs to come after the rules are kept or consequences given. Nurturing is as important as the discipline is, but the timing has to be right. Remember, inconsistent discipline leads to more family confrontations, leading to more stress and more times that mom nurtures her child by breaking rules. This is a vicious cycle that always makes things worse.

The A-Zone always makes things worse. We parents make wrong choices because we literally cannot think straight: in the grip of adrenalin, we cannot sort through our parenting skills to find the best choice for the occasion. We shoot from the hip without aim or thought. We overpower our children with intimidating, drill sergeant actions. By the time 28 minutes has passed, another shot of adrenalin may have resulted from further provocation by the child. Thus, our brains remain in fight or flight mode for an unknown period of time—even overnight, once dysfunctional patterns have been set.

In short: We must know enough to recognize and prevent at least ourselves from straying into a no-win, adrenalin-driven, thoughtless battle. We must be sensitive to our children when they go there. We must be realistic enough to avoid discussions and make an appointment for a future resolution time when anyone is in the A-Zone. *Stress-free Discipline* moves the brain out of emotional discipline into thoughtful discipline, avoiding stress.

Avoid a Vicious Cycle

Discipline is inconsistent and unfair when we allow ourselves to stray into the A-Zone. "Inconsistent" is another word for hypocritical. This closes our child's spirit against us. Our children shut down communication, increasing rebellion and vengeful, negative behavior for hours—perhaps days afterward.

Once the pattern of pain and retreat, rebellion and revenge becomes habit, parents have lost the discipline battle. Parents have also reduced the odds that their child will internalize their faith and values.

Punishment is different from discipline. When they are punished often, children develop resentment and retaliation, and a "Don't get caught," attitude. They view themselves as victims of punishment, and control of that pain is outside of them. They do not feel responsible for punishment coming upon them.

Some parents are "underpowered." They may feel great stress even when they choose to "simply love" their children. These parents believe that if they are patient and lucky, they won't have to do their parenting job at all. Unfortunately, children cannot control their own behavior until we have spent time controlling it for them. As they mature, they internalize those controls. In order for that to happen, we have to exercise gentle but constant control over our children whenever they are immature.

Without a good relationship, discipline degrades into underhanded, barely managed anger. As a result, our children would rather do anything than obey us. They reject our guidance, our values, and our love in a thousand large and small ways. Passive resistance becomes habitual with them. We cannot understand why we are on edge when we should love our little gifts from God.

Realize this: Inconsistent discipline increases the power struggles and testing of our resolve.

Children behave much like mice. A researcher can put mice through a maze with a treat available at the end if the mouse pushes a lever. When the treat is then withheld, the mouse keeps trying the lever a few times and then gives up looking for the reward. However, if a treat is given occasionally, sometimes yes sometimes no, the total times the mouse pushes the lever are greatly increased. The mice remember that they might get a treat.

Likewise, our children who are "rewarded" for breaking a rule (getting off without consequences) will increase their pushy behavior. They will stress us much more than if they never got treats (reinforcement) for misbehavior. Passive parents, write this on your wrist and don't wash. Inconsistent follow-through invites poor behavior.

Pushover parents "love" in a passive way until they are pushed beyond their limits. Inconsistent discipline may include overly harsh, angry or physically rough discipline, unfair application of punishment, changing the deal, or letting the child break rules without giving him or her any consequences. According to 🕮 *The Journal of Abnormal Psychology*, "A large body of literature implicates harsh or overactive discipline as the key causal or maintaining influence on early childhood externalizing problems."[8] Translation: Your angel will probably bite, kick and shove anyone weaker than herself if you don't get discipline right. Angry, over-the-top discipline creates problem behavior. Children remember every unfair move you make.

When poor behavior does not disappear in a month or two in a normal healthy child, it is somehow being rewarded. Our job is to out-think our children and cause their poor choices to evaporate.

Otherwise, repeated patterns of parent-child stress lead to poor quality sleep for everyone every night, and sleep deprivation adds more craziness to already poor discipline.[9] Consider again this question: Is a lifelong love relationship with your child and decent rest important enough to impel you toward organized discipline planning?

In short: We must know when we are caught in a vicious cycle caused by poor discipline. We must be real enough to apologize to our children for our lapse in parenting, to ask their forgiveness and God's grace, and to renew respectful relations with them both.

Eliminate Cultural Stresses

Chaos in society causes stress your parents never experienced. In this culture, good parenting does not come naturally. Poor parenting comes naturally because our media and educational system support us in the poor choices centered on "doing what's right in our own eyes."

Conflict between what is taught at school and in the media with our values at home causes confused, apathetic children. They are likely to adopt a "Whatever!" ethic. They'll try it all depending on the people they are with.

Their internal conflicts cause disobedience and unhappiness at home. This conflict is a major cause of misery, because the children want things that contradict each other.[10] A child cannot please both New Age teachers and traditional, biblically-oriented parents.

Biblical values are trampled in our culture—in public schools, in the media, in our state supported colleges. Delayed satisfactions, sacrifice for the greater good, planning ahead for the benefit of our children, ethical decisions based on the Bible...those choices which cost us everything are all ignored or ridiculed in our New Age culture.

One example is evident in the Harry Potter books. Harry lies and disobeys rules often and receives rewards for that poor behavior, while the students who advocate truth and obedience are ridiculed and unrewarded for their conformity to basic ethical standards. Adult mentors, teachers and influential people in these books disobey their own rules. These books are not fun; they are destructive models for children and should be avoided.

Imitation of this model sows chaos in society. Harry Potter is only one example of our culture's destruction of right values—there is simply no objective standard of right and wrong. Take an informal poll of ten children. Ask them if it is all right to lie, and when. You will be aghast at the results.

In our simplistic culture, feelings control choices. Worse, children are taught that they equal their elders in the right to control their lives and the lives of those around them!

Dr. Thomas Gordon in his course, "Parent Effectiveness Training" expresses this rejection of parental authority in any form. More than a quarter of a million parents have taken his course. His is only one voice which has brought conflict into our families—conflict which never existed in past generations.

Youthful ignorance and enthusiasm is not equal to the wisdom and experience of age. They can be complimentary. They can work together for the benefit of both.

In short: We must know enough about current worldly trends to counter them with God's truth. We must be alert to the "whatever" attitude created by conflict with the world, our child's own desires, and eternally correct principles. We must teach those principles through object lessons, Bible stories, study, discipleship, fellowship, and worship. We must provide godly mentors and find godly peers for our children. This takes time—time you save with *Stress-free Discipline*.

Beware of the High Cost of Permissive Parenting

"Aw, let the kid be a kid." If you have not said it yourself, your spouse or in-law has probably said it to you. This approach assumes that if parents respect and love and serve their children, the children will respect, love and serve their parents. What is left out of this simple approach is the fact that children cannot be self-disciplined unless parents give them good discipline first. Do not teach, explain, exhort first and discipline when you remember it later. Discipline comes first. Respect, love and service require self-discipline and impulse control, which do not come naturally. Myths about discipline are not enough.

Another myth says that in order to be a good disciplinarian, one must be tough, cold and harshly legalistic. On the contrary, a good disciplinarian is warm, relaxed, supportive and nurturing—yes, nurturing—while getting chores done and rules followed. If you're a "natural" at this discipline style, read no further! You are preparing your child for success in school and in his work environments. Your child knows how to stay focused on the task at hand, doing chores quickly and well. As a result your child has fewer behavioral and emotional problems, and no academic problems. However, if you notice challenges in these areas, read on.

Teachers see many problems when students cannot stay "on task." Besides reinforcing poor work habits, time off task builds up over the years. This build-up of failure adds up to school failure for some students, and it limits bright students. The student is, in effect, driving with the brakes on. The failure becomes self-perpetuating. Your child's self-concept suffers horribly.

In short: If we want to produce happy, self-disciplined young adults, we must give them responsibilities and rules as children. The less disciplined our household is, the less success our children will experience in school, among their peers, and in the workplace. We must accept our role as disciplinarians. We must be purposeful and practiced in our parenting technique.

Avoid Stress Caused by Personality Differences

While it is important to respect your child's personality, it is also your job to inspire and require growth fitted to his or her personality, in accord with the Word of God.[11] *Stress-free Discipline* respects personality differences while requiring growth. Note that disagreements about chores may be directly related to personality "glitches."

> If you are requiring your child to be your clone, thinking and acting exactly as you do, you are setting your family up for failure.

Before you make changes, take the time to analyze your personality and that of your spouse. Then consider the children. The Appendix contains a Personality Analysis designed to help you find and understand personality differences that cause family stress. Once you locate problem areas, it is your responsibility to balance or mediate personality conflicts in your family.

Consistent conflict, regardless of what "stage" your child is in, may be based on personality differences that need to be understood and appreciated. Teamwork requires a balance where each person's strengths are useful and respected. It also demands compromise and willingness to sacrifice personal preferences for the benefit of the group. Teamwork is taught, not caught. It does not come naturally. Some people never learn.

Personality differences can make or break family unity depending on when and how they're used. A gift in one setting is a curse in another. Spiritual gifts can be misused. We use them to satisfy our selfish aims rather than to satisfy God's aims. Take the time to become familiar with your different personality styles. Your differences can be well used in the right time, the right way and the right place.[12]

Be careful: The expression of intense or extreme personality differences can fragment or disrupt your family.

This fragmentation can be so severe as to cause divorce or constant arguments. Each member may go off in different directions, working as individuals rather than as a team. Family goals, and the good of the group, are then sacrificed on the altar of "self-fulfillment."

This is not only foolish, but a very poor survival technique to teach your children. If you want to thrive as a family, you must support and encourage the right expression of individual differences. Solitary independent play is not O.K. in mature adults.

Note carefully the basics of personality differences in the Appendix, working through challenges and issues with a counselor as needed. A good counselor will diagnose communication and anger management styles, address problem-solving techniques, and move your family forward as a team. It's no shame to trash bad habits with help from a good counselor.

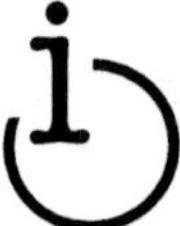

In short: We must know how personality differences impact our family. We must appreciate our differences, respect various approaches to the same problem, and often compromise. We must recognize the problem if it is in our own rigid or unrealistic expectations. This may require counseling. We must be willing to give up our demands for a "comfort zone" based on changing others to be just like ourselves. We must be willing to grow, learning to focus on the benefit of the family, not our self-fulfillment. This prepares our children to succeed in marriage and in the workplace.

Practice "Unnatural" Parenting

Imitating our parents' discipline often fails because of conflict in society, in school and within the family. Good parenting no longer comes naturally. Permissive parenting fails to eliminate a child's poor behavior. Doing what comes naturally is the easy road that leads downhill. On the other hand, excessive authoritarianism often leads to permanently unresolved issues, rebellion and unnecessary use of force by the parent.

There is hope: Poor behavior will disappear when the right discipline is used.

Discipline does not have to be corporal punishment most of the time. Spanking should be used sparingly, and is biblical and useful.[13] Cases of danger or rebellion always call for it—at least up to age six. However, spanking is only a small part of discipline. All discipline must have consistent consequences for specific behaviors.

Consistent consequences do not have to be spanking only. Consequences include down time (early to bed), time out (in a corner), and points off of the time you will spend in fun, educational activities. The key word is "consistent." Consequences may include punishment or—can you believe it?—positive activities.

One example of this truth occurred when my two sons, then ages 12 and 14, sneaked out of our home in the middle of the night. I was making every effort to impose consistent consequences, but it was difficult as a single parent. I was still snoring when they crept out into the frosty Denver night. The full moon and a rumor of satanic rituals in the nearby wheat fields lured them, but chilly boredom brought them back. I woke up in time to catch them as they tried to sneak back into the house. I asked, "What have you been doing?"

I asked that question a lot. If I assumed to know what was happening, I often got it wrong. The ringleader, my eldest, was ready with a bald-faced lie (I learned that ten years later.). "We went out to see the eclipse, Mom, but it was too cloudy." He figured rightly I was a sucker for anything educational. This was a first, and I was unprepared. "We'll have to try again tomorrow night," I said. "How did you know we were gone?" he asked. "I woke up because God woke me! I couldn't hear you breathing!" "You couldn't hear us BREATHING?" Both sons were astonished. "Now get to bed; tomorrow's school." I said.

The next night at 4 a.m. I dragged both warm, sleepy boys out of their beds, herded them blinking and shivering into the car, and went looking for the eclipse. They couldn't say they were not interested, or they would confess to lying. Lying had worse consequences. This was a consistent consequence, but not a planned one. They never sneaked out again. You will have to ask them why.

The consequence was a "positive" one in the sense that no unfounded assumptions on my part, no emotional battles, resulted from their behavior. The consequence had an effect because it frustrated the children and was unpleasant. They really did not want to go out to see the eclipse.

This is my confession to you that there will be unplanned judgment calls where only God can make things turn out right. What's a parent to do? Trust a child until you see he is untrustworthy. Verify when you can. In this case, I had no way of verifying anything, and the natural consequence of roaming around with stray cats and frosted ears had its effect. They said that much. Those boys drove me to prayer such as I had never experienced before.

You will never be a perfect parent. Just remember, the key words are "consistent consequences." You do your best; God does the rest.

Most parents impose consequences only half of the time, causing children to bet on the odds that their misbehavior will go unpunished.

Love has no chance when ineffective discipline is consuming what could be quality times of fellowship and character building. When discipline is haphazard, chaos and emotional stress rule supreme with perhaps hints now and then of grace, growth and love. We hate this, God hates it, yet we are caught up in it if we fail to make a plan and follow through.

In short: We must know what the effects of our "natural, unstructured" parenting will be—confusion, disobedience, and hostility toward our values. We must realize that extreme parenting—either too lax or too rigid, or a combination of both—will not provide the motives our children need to be good. We must be willing to spend quality time with our children, banking love and trust so we can withdraw this love in obedience to our rules.

Find Time for Loving Relationships

Successful parenting requires time. Nagging and doing chores eat up most of the time that parents spend with their children. Children get everything from parents today but quality time. The average father spends three minutes daily speaking to his child—but even that conversation is polluted with orders, criticism and punishment, i.e., "Use your head, Denise!" Teenagers spend an average of three and a half hours alone every day. Sixty-three percent live in households where both parents work outside the home.[14] According to Newsweek, one third of all elementary students return to empty homes.[15] What time children do receive is rarely of a loving quality. They're raised instead by guilt, afterthought, and anger. Everyone then escapes into the hypnosis of television. Nothing is solved, really.

According to Dr. Walt Laramore and Dr. Bill Meier, in a Focus on the Family radio interview (9/18/01 San Diego, California KPRZ 1210 AM radio), there is more and more research detailing the destructiveness of TV. The average TV is on 49 hours per week. It replaces healthy activities, causing more obesity, high blood pressure, violent and poor problem-solving behavior among Americans. Experts suggest we radically trim the number of hours spent with the TV on, and spend those hours with interactive connection with our family. Children are too often abandoned in favor of parents' entertainments.

Feeling unloved, children steal our time with their bad behavior. A smart child often grows up to be a delinquent—gang leaders are most often quite bright.

A Harvard University study identified four crucial factors which prevent future delinquency in young children:[16]

1. The father's firm, fair, and consistent discipline.
2. The mother's supervision and companionship during the day.

3. The parents' demonstrated affection for each other and for the children.
4. The family's cohesiveness—time spent together in activities where all participate.

These are all biblical ideas. God wrote the user's manual for our lives.

Time not spent while children are young is extracted from stressed parents of teenagers in meetings with school officials, probation officers, and other authorities. Desperate parents pay $21,000 per year tuition for military school and add therapy expense, attorney's fees, bail money and damages on top of that. Conflict becomes dirtier with each passing year, until parents kick their children out into the world with a sigh of relief.

Neither parents nor children feel loved. How can we love our children when they are stealing our time with their poor choices? Life is tough enough without that stress. We might as well spend the time early on, saving time and stress later. *Stress-free Discipline* is a time-efficient way to raise loving, productive children. Pay the price (time and effort) now or pay later.

In short: We must be aware of our communication tactics and our distractions. Nagging, sarcasm, criticism and other negatives must be replaced by *Stress-free Discipline* and incentives. We must be willing to spend time and energy learning and practicing loving, supportive discipline techniques. We must spend time in God's Word. We must choose to eliminate or reduce distractions from these goals. Those distractions fragment love. Hebrews 12:1 and 2 have the right recipe for family unity.

Be Aware of Stress Cycles

If your children are constantly testing you, they have been conditioned to obey you only when you are: (1) standing over them, (2) constantly repeating directions and giving them all of your attention, or perhaps (3) screaming at them or hitting them. Only then, they notice, do you really mean it. The rest of the time you are trying to accomplish something else—finish a task, shop for the groceries, talk on the phone, make dinner—and you don't "mean it."

Your distraction means erratic consequences for their poor behavior. They don't help with your chores then, do they? When you aren't looking, they are doing as they please. As they grow, you age. When you want shared goals, they're "doing their own thing." Your family is fragmented. You're a nag. They're escaping responsibility, piling it on you, or getting even for your on-again, off-again discipline in underhanded ways. You're burdened and angry. It's no favor to them to let them have their way, but you're too weary to do otherwise.

There's another source of stress in families. It is called bouncing boundaries. When our children test our limits on their behavior, we have some choices. We may move the boundary (change the rule), enforce the limit (impose consequences), or remove limits altogether.

What effects do these approaches have on children? In one elementary school yard which was surrounded by gentle trees and grassy forest, children chose to play close to the school building when there was no fence which limited them. They were aware of the boundary, but they could not see it. They did not feel free to play near the sunlit forest, even though this was allowed.

However, when a chain link fence was installed on the boundary, the children played right up to the fence. They were happier with a clear limit. They actually felt freer to extend their play toward the forest. Ask yourself: Am I making my children feel safe by bouncing their boundaries all over the place when they test the limits?

Remember that parents stress themselves and their children by reacting to problems rather than preventing problems and by taking time to train themselves in good discipline techniques.

In short: We must understand that it is not kind for us to cause our child stress and to warp our child's perception of authorities (including God) by changing the rules. Doing what comes naturally is not the answer in our anti-family culture.

This book is designed to avoid some of the above pitfalls, giving you...

- A step-by-step plan designed to help you...
- Inspire and train family members to work as a team all the time...
- With the least stress on all of you, thereby...
- Producing better people with better chances for positive long-term relationships.

Create Freedom with Accountability

Effective discipline is not merely punishment. Punishment is less and less necessary once boundaries are clear and consistent. Effective discipline is consistent consequences. The best discipline plan causes family members to work together, not against each other. It has clear, simple rules and goals understood by all. It has realistic expectations for the age level of the child. It will always have appropriate consequences for both poor and good behavior. It will produce healthy, balanced, positive self-esteem in children.[17]

Appropriate boundaries will make your child less likely to be a poor student or even to be victimized when he or she is away from you. A child becomes independent and wise in small steps, supported with the kind of relational and emotional connections our discipline provides.

Poor behavior will disappear as you apply the principles in this book. You will find that your nagging, anger and resentments will also disappear. You will be freed to build positive relationships with your children.

It is interesting to notice that teachers and labor managers must build positive relationships in order to gain cooperation from their students and workers. We all must not only stop undesirable behavior, but motivate people to create quality products and work as a team. Unthinking punishments can give poor results. They can cause people to speed up and produce sloppy work, or slow down and decrease production. The right approach, found in this program, will produce maximum time on task and quality work.

In brief: We must understand and apply the right principles in order to produce maximum, quality effects with minimum stress. We must be self-disciplined and purposeful in order to get good results. True freedom is based on self-discipline.

Free Yourself While You Build Healthy Self-esteem in Your Children

All Heaven breaks loose as children master adult skills. As children grow up with this system, they practice commitment and connections with your values. They learn good work habits, responsibility and cooperation. These skills increase as they grow. Your need of their skills and your appreciation of them is a built-in motivator. Mutual affection blooms. Family members want to "be there" for each other. They are real with each other. They become accountable to each other and to God. Nagging, negative interactions gradually disappear.

When we focus on positive interaction with our children, we prevent the "disconnectedness and alienation that produce so much harm and hurt in kid's lives… We will also impart to them a strong sense of authenticity, security, significance, importance, lovability and responsibility that will equip them to live as children of God."[18]

As I taught "at risk" teens for seven years, I often awoke at 3 a.m. with a restless desire to reach through their rejection of commitment, their separation from society. They despised values I hold dear. I struggled with young drug addicts, fetal alcohol effect teens, gang members, prostitutes and others who had no hope of a positive future. Their future was crime or welfare, and I saw few escape that.

I noticed four common denominators. They were all abandoned by adults who found alcohol, status, entertainment and the god of their appetites more appealing than their duty to their children. Most of the teens felt useless, because they were not part of a family team doing worthwhile activities.

Low self-worth was intensified by lack of skill and discipline. Their pain was almost tangible. They all needed re-parenting, not simplistic self-worth building. They were stuck in a failure cycle. It could happen to your children.

There were remedial students who did succeed. They were the ones who did have a sense of their special worth to their family. They were valuable. Many were living on farms where they worked hard from dawn until dark. They were willing to struggle with reading and math handicaps because they knew they were loved. Parents took time for teaching and discipline—not punishment most of the time, but consistent consequences.

As I worked through *Stress-free Discipline*, names and faces came to mind, urging me forward. I recall asking one misbehaving football player whose father served on the school board, "What would your daddy do if I called him tonight to tell him what you're doing in class?" He said quickly, "He would have me split a cord of firewood and stack it on a hill." "That would take a long time, wouldn't it?" I said. "OH YEAH!" he said. Those consequences were more than he wanted to face. That reminder of consequences—not abuse—was enough to make him a model student the remainder of the term.

> I urge you to make your children your number three priority—after God and your spouse. Whatever their skills and abilities, they must know they are loved and useful. Be proud of every step forward.

As children become more competent through my system, they can help free your time more and more. It's a team effort. You will be chauffeuring them and spending time at their activities. You must teach them adult skills. They must master those skills through repeated practice. As they relieve you, they also free your time. You have time to think. You have time to build quality controls into their learning. They must internalize standards of behavior; you plan for that. The aim for both of you is excellence—"working as unto the Lord."

In brief: We must prevent unhappy and incompetent children by including them in our lives in meaningful ways. We must practice, practice, practice good parenting skills. We must give them our focused attention.

Use and Know Creative, Purposeful Discipline

As your child becomes more competent and conscientious, he learns life skills and becomes more able to compete in the world marketplace.[19] Your children must also learn how to serve you, relate to you, and cooperate with you. Your child's ability and readiness to learn adult skills will please and astonish you. It is a matter of timing—take advantage of small teachable moments spaced throughout the day. Teach them to read early, and accelerate their other skill development with or without teacher's approval. Research shows that the more thinking skills you give to your children, the better they will behave.

I can vouch for that. My hyperactive three-year-old settled down as soon as I began teaching him to read. By first grade he had effortlessly achieved a sixth grade comprehension and reading ability. This move saved my sanity.

Do not listen to the well-meaning kindergarten teacher who tells you not to teach your child to read and write. Watch your child. When he is ready, teach him. Holding children back when they're ready to learn only creates frustration, boredom, learned helplessness, and other bad habits. Children who get a head start stay ahead all the way through school and compete better in the world marketplace. Further, they feel needed and useful.

One Example - Teaching Money Management

Consider involving children early in the process of helping you write checks and balance the checkbook. They can remind you to set aside savings and help you to prioritize your spending when they are teens. You model and teach them important concepts. These same concepts are crammed into one or two classroom hours of Senior Economics class in public schools. Unfortunately, a survey course is useless when students need many hours of practice and discussion. Most of them won't absorb enough financial vocabulary and basic ideas at school to prepare them for success in life.

A three- or four-year-old can learn how you choose what you buy at the market. Unit pricing on the shelf tags can be a learning experience, especially if you give your child a dollar to spend on fruit. At this age they can use a dollar to find a toy at the 99-cent store. The idea is to help them understand real world limits.

When one of my sons was five years old, he scratched his name all over the outside paneling of the preschool building. My consequence was to refinish that. His consequence was to pay a fine—his weekly "donut money" (routinely given by a sweet church senior). He paid in person to the principal for three weeks. While the principal said it wasn't necessary, it did teach a well-remembered lesson. When he was six and bowed in a plate glass window by leaning on it, all I had to say was, "Look at that window bend. If it breaks, that is A LOT of donut money." He jumped away from the window like it was a hot griddle.

Be aware that many states impose severe consequences on parents for their child's misbehavior. Your state may fine or jail you for letting your child participate in gangs. In many states you can be evicted from public housing if your child is using or selling drugs. This is not a complete list, and laws constantly change. I recommend a family trip to the courthouse, jail or D.A.'s office. It is very educational for all of you. Check out the American Bar Association's Division for Public Education (www.abanet.org).

> Crime prevention is all about consistent consequences. One way to teach consequences is to have a mini-jail ministry.

Correspond with a prisoner (of your sex if you're a single parent) and visit him or her with the children. When I did that, one son got everyone's attention in the visiting room by failing the entry scan. The problem turned out to be the arches in his shoes. The notice he received and the impression made by the fences, security and confinement process of the prisoners spoke volumes about consequences. The prisoner was very sorry for all those bad checks he wrote. My children learned a lot about bad checks.

Younger children can be motivated to practice their handwriting and math skills and begin helping you write checks as early as third grade. Yes, your child can write a check to pay the telephone bill, and you can sign it. (You might want to enclose a note for your bank that you're doing this, and initial your child's numbers for the amount.)

Middle school children can help you by working on your home computer entering receipts into QuickBooks or other program for your tax and budget purposes. They can have their own savings account, a source of pride and education.

By fourteen or fifteen, your child should have a checking account, and a debit card, held jointly with you. Together you can teach them "hands on" how to balance their account.

The sixteenth birthday could mean authorized use of a credit card with a minimum credit limit. We want to deglamorize credit. Designer clothing may not be worth six months of payments which total more than the cost of the clothing and the temporary status they bring at school.

Relevant chores teach impulse control

As your children watch how you spend money, you can say things like, "I felt like buying that dress for myself, but I knew you needed shoes more, so I controlled my impulse and bought your shoes." Children will gain a wider understanding of impulse control as you bring them into the world of adult responsibilities. Their self-worth will be based on real accomplishment as they gain a long-term view of life. That same long-range view of life will help them avoid the "fast fun" errors of their peers when they are teens.

Two heads are better than one. The chores you hate may be fun for you both when your children are helping. Here's where that youth and enthusiasm for adulthood can shore up your tired age and experience. This is a big adventure. Your child's eyes may sparkle at the chance to help you, but if your chores replace a media addiction, do not be surprised at a lack of enthusiasm.

Try to make chores fun even when you hate them, since your emotional baggage will weigh heavy on your children when they're adults doing the same chores. You should set an example of someone who enjoys the price of adult freedoms.

If you're blessed with a child opposite to your personality, he or she may even help you enjoy your worst chores by enlarging your skill set. Two heads really do end up being better than one.

Using complimentary skills is a bonding experience. This is practice for lifelong teamwork.

Do not be afraid to make mistakes and admit it. Have your child check your work and make a few deliberate errors so you can be corrected. If your child gets too cocky about correcting you, tell her you were just testing her. You can share a good laugh when she doesn't believe you. Relax and be real. When you make a genuine mistake, your child will think you did it on purpose! Joyous teamwork is the goal. It is biblical to enjoy your work. Ephesians says joy in your labor is a gift from God.

If you're authoritarian to an extreme, your "perfection" leads toward your child's blind acceptance of any authority—right or wrong. Do not worry about being perfect. Work on being biblical.

Use imagination breaks to balance work with play. When working with your child on difficult tasks—the checkbook or bank balance, for example—take frequent breaks (every 10-15 minutes) to avoid burnout. Take an imagination break. Get up from the checkbook table and pretend for three minutes to be picking peaches. Stand high on tiptoes, and imagine the smell of the trees, the feel of the sun and the breeze, etc. Imagine throwing peaches at each other, if you really want to be rowdy. Then imagine cleaning up the mess! Clown around. Then have the child create the next imagination break. Make it physical, pantomime, using or imagining the use of all five senses.

In brief: We must read as much as we can, exchange ideas and practice with a learning partner in order to make a child approach adult skills with pleasure. Otherwise we get children stuck in a Peter Pan Syndrome (I don't want to grow up). Reading skills and money (read that math skill) management are two essential adult skills which need to be taught early.

Strategy: Master Truly Effective Discipline

How do you know when your discipline is effective? If your children are obeying you in the short term, will you have good relationships years from now?

Consider these marks of ineffective discipline:

- You are exhausted, irritated and always on the defensive.
- Things are not improving.
- You feel like a boss facing a labor shutdown.
- You are cynical and ready to give up.
- You are quick to enter the "A-Zone."
- You are rationalizing away your child's poor behavior.

- You are bribing your child so he will not misbehave in public.
- You use punishments quickly while others are getting good behavior from their children without using punishment.
- Your children only behave well when you are watching.
- You do not sleep well.

If you have reached this sorry state, realize the difference between this condition and good discipline. Truly effective discipline provides consistent consequences with additional motivation. You set limits, stopping undesirable behavior. You also provide the right reinforcement and motivation to start correct behavior.

Good discipline is not the same as punishment, and does not have to include physical pain most of the time. Never spank a child when you're really angry, but give yourself time to cool off and gather your wits. You do not want to be abusively harsh. Punish your child with down time in a corner until you can cool down.

Effective discipline means frustrating the child rather than the parent. Preventing a child from doing what he or she wants is often the only "punishment" needed.

➥ Do not be afraid of angering and frustrating your children.[20] Your job is to teach them life skills that actually work in the real world. "Frustration tolerance" is an essential skill. Moreover, frustration often takes the place of physical pain. It is often more effective in teaching a child to follow rules. Rule-following behavior is a good survival technique for both adults and children.

Children learn to be responsible when they do chores "just because" they are members of your family. Spoiling your children, requiring little of them, fails to teach them responsibility. It also gives them a warped view of the world and a selfish mind set which you'll have to "re-teach" later—amid violent protest. It is not love to let a child have control when you should have control. A balance of control and love will produce a balanced child.

The most effective discipline keeps a child watching his or her own behavior with minimal stress once the system is in place.

Effective discipline will cause the bad behavior to self-destruct, not get worse. It also rewards right behavior, produces terrific self-esteem and aids the socialization and concept-development process. All of these are essential to good parenting. None can be left out without leaving the parenting job poorly done.

> Finally, effective discipline must be consistently, fairly applied and be free from emotional reactions on the parent's part.

If you think you cannot do this, consider the alternative. If you avoid confrontation by letting your child do as he/she wants, you cause more stress—long-term—than it's worth.[21] This stress creates family discord that can trigger mental illness in your child or you! Besides, your adrenals can only take so much before your body wears out. Good work now gives you energy to play with your grandchildren later.

If you glorify your family traditions of authoritarian (knee-jerk) discipline, ask yourself whether your grandparents were calm because they had a wise view of life or because their adrenals were exhausted from poor discipline practices with your parents!

Effective life skills cannot be "caught;" they must be taught. You, the adult, must not only inspire right choices and self-discipline, you must enforce them until the child is mature enough to be proactive and self-disciplined on his or her own. That is your job. Like all jobs, it is more frustrating and difficult if you don't have the right skills and tools. This book is designed to give you both.

In brief: We must recognize when our discipline is useless or when it is actually rewarding poor behavior. Children will naturally resist doing chores and following rules, but the little children are our responsibility. A balance of love and control will produce a balanced, controlled child.

Internalize the Goals of Discipline

The goal of parental discipline is to teach interdependent, skillful family relationships and to produce self-reliant, mature children. Let's take a careful look at what that means.

Interdependence is different from independence. We need to keep this clear in our thinking. Independence has been stressed in our culture, often at the expense of being able to work as a team. Team players are the most valuable workers and family members, not loners. I know of a Mensa (awesome) intellectual who was fired from a high-powered job because he lacked teamwork skills.

Interdependence means the person has the skills to accomplish his/her task alone—be independent—but may freely choose to do this as part of a team. The independent person is able to accomplish a task without any outside help but may not freely choose to work as a team with anyone. Loners—even brilliant loners—are not wanted in the job market or in marriages.

➥ Self-reliant children may have all the skills to be independent, but parents, your work is not done. Your smart, capable children may not be able to work as a team for the enhancement of the lives of those around them. Without your help, they grow from selfish children into selfish adults, incapable of lasting, socially responsible marriages. Thus, interdependence is the ultimate goal of successful parenting.

Much of current self and family-improvement literature places independence above teamwork, self-sacrifice, and true maturity. Misguided "experts" call teamwork and commitment "co-dependence." Adult children are told to "Look out for number one."

The result is that people "fulfill themselves" by leaving their jobs or family commitments, abandoning children to the grief and trauma of fragmented families and cursing them with poor odds for happy marriages themselves. These people have impulse control problems. *Stress-free Discipline* teaches impulse control one step at a time.

In brief: We must help children learn teamwork "just because" they are part of a family. We must resist any efforts to focus on "self-fulfillment" at the expense of service. A servant mentality is the humble and contrite heart which God loves. Remember that Eve fell when she took her eyes off the goal (service to God) in favor of self-fulfillment.

Build Teamwork: Healthy Interdependence

What does healthy interdependence look like? Interdependent people choose to work as a team while alone they are self-reliant and capable. They know that teamwork can accomplish far more than one person can accomplish alone.

Emotionally interdependent people understand the need for loving and sharing with others while at the same time they are happy with whom they are as individuals.

Intellectually interdependent people aren't reinventing the wheel; rather, they work with others, gaining the brilliance of other lights besides their own. At the same time they are avoiding their own pitfalls and blind spots. A joy that's shared is a joy made double. Stress that is shared is stress cut in half! Joy is multiplied, stress reduced.

> Interdependent people find synergistic joy in teamwork.

For example, a group of farmers tested their draft horses to see which could haul the largest loads. They piled weights on a sledge attached to their horses. They found that the strongest horse could pull nine tons. The runner-up hauled seven tons. Curious, they teamed the horses, expecting the team to pull sixteen tons. That did not happen. Rather, the team pulled 32 tons! The team had synergistic effects, encouraging and supporting each other to accomplish together much more than each horse could do alone.

A healthy interdependent family will have many team victories amid the stresses of everyday life. This is a great joy we may otherwise miss. It forms a lasting love connection with your children after they are grown.

Dad, we know you're tired at night, but family interdependence is too important an issue for you to avoid.[22] You can pick up your newspaper and dirty socks, help make your bed, and so forth. Remember: interdependence—teamwork—is the goal!

Dad, when you reward your child for good behavior, good things happen to your body. When you spend time with your knee-hugger after work, you will experience a legal high. Your weary bones will be energized with endorphins, the brain chemicals which kill pain and inject joy. Those chemicals are 400 times more powerful than morphine. Moreover, you are brought into God's favor because you are nurturing and educating your child. TV cannot compete with those energizing blessings.

Dad, do not disrespect your wife and daughters, especially by refusing to cooperate with them (work) in creating a fine home. If you "dis" your wife with your put-downs, do not expect your daughters to embrace the roles of homemaker, wife and mother. Do not expect your son to respect women if you cannot cooperate with a plan for the entire household. Because you're the chosen leader, God expects more of you.

Check out Dr. James Dobson's book, 🕮 *Bringing Up Boys*, for details on how essential good fathering is, especially for boys. Your boy will suffer if Dad is not actively involved. Fathers are especially needed to teach appropriate anger management, sex roles, sublimation and impulse control.

Impulse control and other adult skills are necessary for family "team" victories. Without self-mastery, as Dr. Steven R. Covey brilliantly details in his book, 🕮 *The Seven Habits of Highly Effective People*, interdependence is impossible.[23] Imagine your child, then, winning private victories in your home that build up his strength of character to that satisfying place where he can have public victories and praise.

Impulse control is in the first, elementary set of expectations for your child, tot or teen. This book helps you create self-mastery in your child and joyful interdependence in your family.

In brief: We must build joy and reduce stress through healthy teamwork (interdependence). The best way for us to accomplish this is through study, prayer and practice. Our rewards may not show right away. This is a marathon, not a sprint. They do show up in long-term love and respect and teamwork long after the children are adults.

Beware of Myths and Mistakes in Discipline

We have mentioned some of the errors and terrors of poor discipline, but there are a few other mistaken ideas which we need to address.

Many discipline systems gain the child's cooperation, but they cost us too much time to be worth our while. One of these is the old standby, behavior modification. By the time we buy and distribute enough small toys and other motivators of good behavior, we are exhausted and cranky.

These "costs of being parents" are tricky, since we may not realize that our system is not working. If the poor behavior recurs often over a period of months, we need to know that what we are doing is not working. Good discipline causes poor behavior to go away.

> A second mistake parents make is to believe that only the big crises require discipline. In fact, the most important discipline problems are the small, frequent ones which will not go away.

Failure to stop that behavior leads to more and more pushing of our boundaries. Our children then bet that we will also ignore the bigger misbehaviors.

- These power struggles kill our love for our children by degrees. We become chronically tired, depressed, short tempered, and eventually physically ill.[24]

Parents give up trying to control minor disruptions convinced that it's just a little thing. They even let children fight it out between them. Realize that small, frequent problems can be controlled without turning you into a raving lunatic.

Thirdly, frustrated parents ignore small problems, ask children to stop misbehavior, and then are fooled by the child's charm or other ploys. Parents then ask children to stop again when the problem recurs, finally laying down the law in a thundering fit, all in the mistaken belief that this will cause the child to behave. In fact, small problems grow into big ones when they are ignored.

Fourth, tired parents give up proactive discipline on the theory that love, grace, teaching and learning magically provide all their leverage for enforcing rules. Not true. Parents, you are in the discipline game every waking minute. Be proactive—act like a pro. A pro rewards every step toward the right goal, and imposes consequences for every small step away from the right goal every waking minute.

- Children feel uninspired because they do not receive emotional rewards or time with their parents when they are behaving well. In fact, grace in the "love bank" helps us enforce rules. Love is spelled T-I-M-E.

Fifth, parents figure that the child should know how to behave from one brisk, often fuzzy teaching session. This is false. The only thing you know for sure after you have taught your child is that he will forget some of what you want him to know. We must carefully teach and re-teach, but there is a right and a wrong way to do this. We must either spend time and effort (learning, practicing, and doing) in the beginning of our discipline process, or we will be spending a lot more painful effort and time as the children grow up.

The Stress-free Discipline system has been carefully designed to avoid the above pitfalls.

Children find this system a good game in itself. They express natural rivalry with creative, positive point-getting, rather than by hostility, tattling, nagging and manipulative put-downs. You won't have to watch them every second once the good system is established. Poor behavior will evaporate. You won't have to nag, scream, raise your blood pressure or lose sleep.

In brief: Behavior modification and letting small issues slide are ineffective discipline systems. We must know the myths of discipline so we can see when we slip into bad habits. We must practice effective discipline until it becomes easy and fun.

Grasp the Big Picture

Stress-free Discipline includes five sets of stage-appropriate expectations and separate point charts. I created the expectations using my experience in creating scope and sequence curricula for students. These task lists include maximum performance criteria—the best your child can be. They have built-in flexibility, since you may change them as you wish. For example, you may wish to add various good-manners tasks, such as saying, "please" and "thank you," while I have not listed them. (Score manners under Impulse Control.) Just make certain that your expectations have been made very clear. Your child succeeds when expectations are drilled until they become easy to perform.

- ➥ The point charts help you track both positive and negative performance. Points are written in stone; leave them unchanged.

Points are time you will spend in fun, educational activities with your children. You award grace points in advance. You do not have to relieve stress by changing rules or inventing new consequences.

This system is flexible enough to allow you to discipline your children as individuals, groups or teams. Since you reward your child with quality time with you, it is possible to reward individuals (breakfast out with Dad?) or the whole flock or teams. Your educational activities may include building social skills, sports skills (call it kinesthetic education), music education (concerts), spiritual events or academics.

Skill Mastery and Flexible Expectations

Your child's mastery of a chart may or may not coincide with the age levels on the Expectations Charts. A highly motivated or precocious child may move rapidly through the charts...a less mature one much more slowly. It is possible that a three-year-old may have remained on Chart 1 for two to four years before mastering the expectations. Do not worry. Late bloomers may be more consistent in the long run.

You are the best judge of your child's competence and so will tailor the expectations to your family needs.

I suggest that when you begin a new list, you simplify your expectations by taking on the hardest tasks yourself. Gradually, those harder tasks will be included in the child's list as you see the child's skills grow. You may want to add specific good manners, specific negotiation skills, or other items to the basic household responsibilities on the Expectations Lists. The Point Charts will accommodate any expectations under their general categories.

- ➥ This is not a contest. The only competition is with one's own best self.

When one Expectations List is mastered you will celebrate, then move on to the next higher level. Rewards or benefits for mastery of each list may include various gifts from you. Favorite clothing, vacation from chores for a day or a week, toys, a party, a trophy, later bedtime, raise in allowance, more game or sports time...these will motivate your child toward excellence in moving from one level to the next higher one. For example, "graduation" benefits for a three-year-old who has mastered the chores in Chart 1 might include a field trip, a circus performance, special treat food...just make the benefit fit your budget, with an eye toward keeping it simple. You do not want to start a rewards program that you cannot follow for years to come.

The point charts have been inspired by the best classroom management system ever developed: the Fred Jones "Positive Classroom" instructional and management system.[25] Extensive research and development went into Dr. Jones' system. I have extrapolated principles from that research for use in parenting. I have synthesized the rest of this time-effective system from my own research and lessons learned in 19 years of teaching and parenting.

Materials

You will need a stopwatch, copies of the enclosed lists and charts, scrap paper and a clipboard. Charts that will fit a 9" x 12" clipboard are enclosed.

Weekly Motivators

A section on motivators has a few games and other ideas useful in rewarding positive behavior. You may want to brainstorm high interest enrichment ideas with your child in advance of the weekly or daily rewards event. Take your children shopping at the nearest teacher supply store.

Choose something which the children genuinely want. It must be educational, perhaps object lessons teaching the difference between right and wrong, sports skills, social skills, musical or academic skills.[26]

- Reward games must be something educational that parents can live with.

Built-in Motivators

Stress-free Discipline awards more points for using a technique, rather than stiff penalties for failure. It also gives grace points up-front. Those things are very important. Do not change the points. Success breeds success.

➥ Take the time to practice this system every day for 32 days. That's how long it takes to break bad habits and establish good ones. Your self-discipline will be richly rewarded.

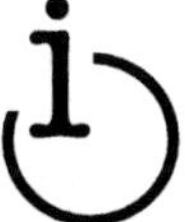

In brief: There's nothing brief about a marathon. Good discipline is not a sprint, it's a marathon.

Reinforce Goal-driven Choices

Your own relief and pleasure will help you reinforce your specific parenting process. There are other ways to make sure you stay with your program. First, pray your priorities and resist any temptation to fall out of the pattern of this discipline. Follow the pattern every day, vacations or school days, and you will not have to start over. Resist every temptation to do it halfway. Just as a recipe requires every part to be done, so this system requires complete follow-through.

Happiness is skillful parenting.

According to current happiness research, you'll be most happy when your ability and the task at hand are closely matched.[27] *Stress-free Discipline* brings your skill level from the reactive, amateur level up to the proactive, mastery level. Skillful parents enjoy their parenting chores. This reinforces your right choice to pursue this program.

Second, child discipline has been researched and field-tested. You do not have to do original research! Amateur parenting—inconsistent, inefficient or misguided discipline—is stressful original research. Research takes plenty of time and a large research sample to produce valid results. You do not have to reinvent effective parenting. You will get results without tedious research.

➥ A byproduct of *Stress-free Discipline* is your own happiness. Progress will make you healthier, more creative, productive and altruistic.[28]

Third, your relief from the emotional baggage which goes with unskilled parenting will astonish and please you. If you suffer from depression, realize that 30-50 percent of depression is caused by poor self-esteem. Your self-esteem takes a bad blow when your children misbehave. For your own sake, skillful parenting is a must.

Repeat after me: "For my own sake, I have to be a skillful parent."

Fourth, mastery of parenting skill brings rewards: One of them is that you have answers to your child's challenges. When your children press you for adult freedoms too early, you point to their performance on adult skills, then to your own specific expectations for yourself. Let them know that their adult freedoms come at the price of mastery of Youth Expectations 5 (for ages 14-18.) By this time in your relationship, they are aware of the skills you lack. They are helping you to quit smoking, eat 5-9 servings of fruits and vegetables a day, exercise regularly and change other bad habits.

Fifth, a team spirit evolves out of this program. You are not strutting around lecturing your children with worthless generalities. You are being real. They understand exactly how skillful you both are, and what you both have to learn. You have eliminated a divisive, ongoing source of conflict between you. You have built a lifelong love bond.

Discuss with them where they are in their mastery of adult skills. Mastery skill level is not the same as beginning level. Mastery means doing a task well and quickly.

Sixth, this system helps children understand precisely where they are in the growing process. If they are not fast, effective, complete and neat in getting chores done, they have not mastered the chores. Chores do not start being fun until they are mastered. Reread the four paragraphs above this one!

Seventh, your children will want this system. They learn that they cannot be happy as adults if they are incompetent.

> Note that the significant increase of depression and suicide in children and teens is related to skill levels. Poor self-esteem is directly related to poor skills.

Eighth, authority and responsibility develop hand-in-hand. We are responsible for our children; we must exercise authority over them. As time passes they become responsible for themselves, mastering adult chores. Then they qualify to assume more and more authority over their own lives.

Finally, advanced levels of *Stress-free Discipline* build advanced skills in both you and your children. Beyond the marketable skills of team play and advanced concept development, there are negotiation skills. Once basic good habits are established with older children, try working week by week through a negotiating techniques book such as the classic 🕮 *Getting to Yes*, by Roger Fisher, William Ury and Bruce Patton of the Harvard Negotiation Project.[29] You can take each technique and apply it to conflicts between family members in a group role-playing session. Points will be awarded for seeing the conflict from the other person's point of view. This is one educational game that anyone can use.

I also recommend Dr. Jones' teaching seminars and weekend workshops. They teach you how to teach any skill. This book has some teaching tips, but in-depth training is beyond my scope here.

In brief: Happiness is skillful parenting. Skills take time, work, sacrifice, and focus. Like true Christianity, this system is simple but not easy.

Understand Biblically-based Authority

If we live in the Spirit, let us also walk in the Spirit.

Galatians 5:25

This discipline system has an unusual component. It strikes a balance between the authoritarian, "I walk on water" discipline that requires unthinking, instantaneous obedience from children of all ages toward their parents, and the liberal, anti-authority views of misguided child advocates.

> *Stress-free Discipline* requires real world progress based on wise use of authority, truth and mutual respect.

It is a fact that "...demanding unquestioning obedience from children goes beyond what (Jesus) instructed...Authoritarianism goes beyond healthy, positive discipline and demands absolute submission."[30] I agree with Ms. Ramer that "Many children who receive this type of 'training' grow up to fear their parents and any adult figure."

I believe such "training" teaches a child to submit to wrongful dominance as adults. It is hard to "retrain" an intimidated person. An intimidated child grows into an adult who probably will not stand up to aggressive, wrongful behavior.

I have raw data and a report done by a licensed private detective on Bible-based, authoritarian cults. These cults prey on Christian children successfully because the family love bonds are weak. The family love bonds are weak because they are based on unquestioning obedience to authority. This is dangerous!

Parents sometimes see their use of authority as "Either I'm in control or out of control." This is incorrect. Parental authority is a continuum, a balance that we maintain always in a spiritual sense (honor your father and mother) but dynamic—in motion—in a practical sense. We give up our control little by little as we work ourselves out of the parenting job. We give control more and more to our children as they master life skills. They are thus well prepared for adulthood when they reach eighteen.

We need a dynamic balance of power, growth and control: We cannot afford to be passive. We need a plan.

That is why this system sports a dual purpose Parents' Expectations Chart. Let's face it, most parents reach adulthood with unresolved issues which are important but not urgent enough to compete with the everyday "crises" of raising children. Long-term issues, which can cause great pain in a person's life, recede into the Never Never Land of low priority.

Children's issues, on the other hand, are compelling and immediate. Thus, a parent's unresolved stress becomes an obstacle to fulfilled living for both parents and children. Bad habits, such as failure to deal with financial realities, become habitual in stressed parents, reducing their quality of life and cheating them of joy in parenting. I suggest you can simply resolve this dilemma. (Note, I did not say easily solve the problem. Growth and change is never easy.)

One purpose of the Parents' Charts is to inspire you to grow out of your chronic long-term dysfunctions. The second purpose is to help your children avoid living out your problems. Use the Parents' Point Chart and your choice of Parental Expectations for yourself. Encourage your most mature child to help you with your problem-solving process.

Before you carry through on this idea, you will want to analyze which challenges you want your child to help you overcome. If you have trouble getting all your chores done, consider your time management and expectations for yourself.

- ➥ Discuss your priorities with your children. They may help you make a target correction you don't think is needed. What are really the most important things for you to do?

Review the sample Parents' Expectations and prioritize your chores for the purpose of balancing your life. A priority matrix—a skeleton form—to aid you in this task is in the Appendix.

Ask yourself: Do I have an impossible picture of the perfect parent I want to be? Am I emotionally overwhelmed? Do I have impulse control problems my children will imitate if I do not change? Am I depressed and angry because of frustrations or stresses? Am I caught up in a vicious cycle with no way out? Do I need to arrange a simplified life?

Now ask yourself: Have I run myself ragged chasing small disruptions and rule violations without having the problem go away? Or, have I given up on this, allowing small fires of disorder to grow into major wild fires of conflict? Have I given up on myself—on caring for the temple of God? Your body needs maintenance, nurturance, and revitalization in all areas of life. Are you balancing your spiritual needs, emotional and thought life, and physical care?

Have you given up on discipline, on being consistent, on being tough and on trying harder? Who will help you stay on track? Have the important long-term issues been immersed in a flood of small, urgent issues? As my mother once said, "The problem with life is that it is so daily!"

- ➥ Are your priorities erased by distractions? Eliminate the joy-stealing cares of this world which choke out biblical living.

If you are exhausted in the struggle, you are in good company—but the solution is not cheap. The answer requires your attention, time and effort.

Pay the price early, or pay a higher price later.

But who will help you with quality control of your own parenting skills? Perhaps you are a single parent, a military spouse, or just on the scene more than your husband is. He comes home stressed, tired, and not thinking beyond the "quick fix of punishment." What is the wise course? How do you both perfect your skills?

Perfect Your Skills —Be Accountable

Your growth and family discipline is a life and death issue—an abundant life or spiritually dead lifestyle issue. Without doubt Christ is the answer to all our problems. Unfortunately, He does not have skin on. Your learning partner is part of your answer. Find a God-centered learning partner who irritates you by thinking differently from the way you think. Meet regularly. Talk daily on the phone. Speak the truth in love.

Spend the time now in learning and practice. Practice those new parenting skills until you no longer have to think about them. Practice until they become automatic. Practice with your learning partner and your spouse and caregivers.

Beyond that, who is on your home scene, intimately involved in your daily choices? Your child would enjoy keeping you on target by awarding you points when you do your job well. At the same time, your child is learning functional adult skills without enrolling in the school of hard knocks.

Furthermore, when your child gives you more positive points than negative ones, good things happen. He sees:

- What a tough assignment from God parenting really is.
- What a good job—overall—you are really doing.

- How important your issues are to his future happiness.
- Be real. You will get more respect!

If you do not take this opportunity, ask yourself, "Exactly how will I unlearn my bad habits? How much time and money do I have for counseling?"

If you wish to lose weight or quit smoking, this is your chance. How about that scripture memory program you keep resolving to do? A parents' chart system helps you stay on target, changing for the better, within the limits you set. At the same time your children learn by watching you. You may squirm a bit, but your child will enjoy helping you. Do not worry about undermining your authority. Your child already knows your weak spots, and will admire your good modeling of cheerful, proactive problem solving. Do not wait for a crisis before you change yourself. Crisis management is exciting, but not efficient.

Crisis management is stressful and not nearly as productive as well thought out change. Remember the non-thinking A-Zone? Is your life a drama without sense? Is it full of sound and fury, meaning nothing? Growth is up to you.

Your family relationships will change as you model honesty and growth. Forgiveness and truth will bring everyone into compassionate, lifelong love relationships. Your children will respect your leadership, even though they may chafe under it. While you overcome your own weaknesses with their help and this parenting tool, your children are gaining self-worth and learning adult skills.

Be Proactive

A well thought-out schedule is the only way you will be happily successful in our warp-speed, multi-tasking world. If you feel stressed, are you trying to do too much? Are your standards appropriate only if you had a full-time maid? Successful parenting means you will prioritize and do each of your own chores with time management in mind. Many books detail efficient housework routines and other time saving procedures. You and your children can cut hours off your chore time with time saving methods.

In short: You can maintain authority while asking for help on specifics where you need help. It is a pity when our pride prevents us from building interdependence—when we feel we must protect our image at all costs. This is a dysfunctional attitude. Dysfunctional families are dishonest. They lie, creating falsehoods to maintain an illusion—an image—of being perfect. They keep secrets. This is not workable. There's a better answer.

Accountability unifies your family under Christ as the head. Children need to be an important, useful part of our lives. They do not deserve to be under-rated or put down when they are truly capable. They do not deserve to feel like a burden to you because you have made them dependent on you for everything! Listen to me. They need your growing measure of respect for what they can do for the family. They definitely need practice in making judgments, in the dynamics of control and cooperation. It's a complex world. Holding you accountable is practice for their successful adulthood.

Real world discipline does not make the world safe for the child by protecting or isolating him. It trains his discernment and then allows him to make choices—choices that begin small and grow step-by-step with the child. This is wisdom.

Model Assertiveness, Not Aggression

Consider the difference between aggression and assertiveness. Aggression toward your child is based in hostility and dominance. It will model all the wrong things to your children—anger management problems, impulse control problems, power grabs. Aggression is taking action against a person. Your job is to take action against the sin, not the sinner. Assertiveness is the Christ-like model because love was always Christ's motive (see Luke 9:51-56).

➥ While Jesus lived assertively, He chose at times to be aggressive (when He threw money-changers out of the temple) and to be passive (when He allowed the rich young ruler to leave sorrowing over the price of discipleship.)

The fact that Christ took no action toward the rich young ruler allowed him to choose his own future. Christ suffered great grief to watch that young man condemn himself by his own choice.[31] To be passive is to suffer, to take no action, and to be unresisting.

There will be times when you will deliberately risk your child's failure by being passive, in order to allow your child to make his own choice and to grow. Clearly, you will not allow life-changing horrible consequences, but will match the free choice you allow to the maturity of your child.

You will have to balance your behavior according to the need. Your self control will be the best Bible your children ever read.

When you have made a Christ-like choice, explain it to your child. You might say, for example, "When you disobeyed I felt like spanking you, but I was so upset and angry I might have hurt you. I choose to give you a time-out instead." You might say, "I am so angry now I can't think straight. I'll punish this when I calm down." You thus model sound mind thinking—a balanced, proactive approach to problem solving.[32]

➥ Real world discipline will allow a child to express his or her feelings (respectfully), but inhibit the kind of impulse control problems which result in unacceptably harmful behavior.

It is normal to become angry when frustrated, hurt or fearful.[33] Children must be taught what their feelings are and taught how to express them without harming others. They must be allowed to be angry without sinning!

A child must learn to be assertive in order to develop the skills he will need in a highly competitive society. This does not mean the child is allowed to take control of the family by what he says or does. When your child tries a wrongful grab for your authority, just remind him that you are the coach and the quarterback, and God owns the team. Give word pictures for your roles, and he will accept them more easily. Your daughter may be a princess, but you're the king or queen.

Our goal, then, is to raise Bereans.

Bereans are the Christians who are deep thinkers—who test what they hear and see for validity against the scriptural truth we all accept. We do not want knee-jerk, "Yes, Ma-am!" intimidated children to grow into mediocre adults with no ability to analyze—to spot counterfeit from the genuine. That's why it is important to teach your children to measure your behavior, their behavior, and all other influences against the Word of God. Iron sharpens iron.

➥ Children need to have maturity-related, significant control of family dynamics within defined boundaries. Your job is to gradually increase their choices as your "letting go" process unfolds.

This helps them grow into responsible, self-reliant adults. It is far easier to "let go" of controlling their every move in small steps. You choose the area of change; you orchestrate the forward motion, teaching all the way.

➥ If you do not control their independence in small steps of your choice, they will take choice away from you. They will rebel and take ignorant, total control in a crisis of their own creation.

Mom, those boys will strut center stage and demand control. Daughters use less obvious maneuvers to get their way. They both must be made to understand early that adulthood means freedom with responsibility and self-control. You will grant them more freedoms (such as later bedtime) when they show more responsibility.

In brief: The rightful exercise of authority does not come naturally for most of us. Parenting requires us to be thoughtful, eliminating urgent distractions in favor of long-term, important goals. We must pray our priorities before God, discuss them with our families and Christian mentors, and continuously check our own quality of parenting by watching our family dynamics.

Maintain Your Accountability

The Parents' Chart and Expectations system helps parents stay on target while helping children learn by watching. As we resolve our difficult issues, our children learn the right behavior early, avoiding the vicious cycle of "inheriting" our faults. Do not worry. The "control" over us that our children take when Parents' Charts go into effect does not diminish our authority. We only give children the task of keeping us accountable on a limited basis. We decide the boundaries. (Remember: no discussion, no debate.)

Readiness is all: Begin the Parents' Point Chart 1 one month after you begin your child's Chart 1 (or later as you see fit). At that time, give one child in your family the clipboard with your Expectations (one chore) and Parents' Point Chart 1 only if your child wishes to do this. When you begin, you will have one simple chore for your child to help you monitor. This avoids confusion on the child's part. Later, when and if your child wishes to expand his or her role, list two chores you need reminders about. In the beginning we make those chores literal and tangible; that's how your child thinks. The more difficult tasks—those that take higher order thinking skills—will come later.

If more than one child wants to have a hand in helping you, pass the clipboard from one to another child on a rotation of once every month. You are not forcing your children into adult roles, since your child can resign this voluntary position any time. On the other hand, a lot of good things happen when children learn about adulthood by playing adult roles. *Stress-free Discipline* is designed to give children brief insights—step by step—into your responsibilities.

Fairness: Children have a strong sense of what's fair. It is fair for both parents and children, in fact, to hold themselves to the standard of accountability to God. It is fair for all family members to measure their performance with biblical standards. It is not fair to say we are Christians if we are not practicing our faith daily with our family. Practice does make perfect.

What would Jesus do? He reserved for Himself the judgment that was His right, yet did not coerce obedience and commitment from the Pharisees and other critics. Let us ask ourselves, are we unnecessarily coercing our children? Are we following Jesus as we raise them? Are we equipping them or stripping them of incentive by threats?

How are we teaching our children true maturity? While punishment is a part of discipline, as each child matures our need to punish in order to enforce rules must mature as well. The need for punishment will eventually evaporate. Our children will be self-controlled. *Stress-free Discipline* seeks to follow Jesus' example of love while keeping our duties clear and our authority intact.

As parents we tend to "let up" pressure on ourselves to confess our own sin and change our behavior. Our children, however, are watching all the time and they do not forget. They judge us and they imitate us.

They grow up to marry people with our flaws, subconsciously hoping to fix their family-of-origin problems. Thus, our flaws become our legacy. No! No!

We must not presume upon God's grace by doing whatever we want, whenever we feel like it. Remember Ananias and Sapphira.

Remember the priest Eli, held accountable for ignoring sins committed by his two sons (see 1 Samuel). We have a responsibility not only to change and challenge ourselves, but also to raise children who are willing and able to transform our culture.

Our challenge is to create "Revelationary" changes in our own family. In order to change, to redeem our culture, we must interact with it and with our children in a thoughtful way. No matter how active the Revelation churches were, the only two that did not have God's criticism were those two which were persecuted and evangelical. What type of Christians are we? Will our children master our faith?

We are not persecuted yet.[34] I hope we are evangelical in focus. Let us choose to study and change, debate and think through our activities that are so often automatic and incomplete. Let us resolve to think through all of our responsibilities with an eye toward reducing those of low priority—in God's eyes. I pray this program will help you do just that, replacing the low priority chores with the highly important, faith-based, healthy family activities which will draw others to Christ.

In brief: We are accountable to God and to our children. We owe our children the best part of us. We teach our children by our behavior and how to solve problems or how to ignore them until they become a crisis. We teach them ethical behavior, how to prioritize, how to cheerfully exercise adult freedoms. We all learn on the job—lifelong lessons. What would Jesus do? The Parents' Charts help you grow while your child is useful and feels needed.

What does this parental accountability look like?

Here's a mini-drama to show you how it works. While boundaries are important, there is still space for grace. Grace is built into the point system to start each day. You give grace up-front. You do not have to decide for grace or law every time a rule is broken. Use law when the rules are broken. Remember, too many warnings with too few tickets creates chaos.

Submitting to One Another in Love: Balancing Law and Grace

Characters: Susan, thirteen years old; Mike, eleven; Mom; Dad, and Narrator. Mom and Mike each have clipboards and stopwatches.

Mom: (Losing her temper, on her high keys, points her clipboard at Susan) "I've really had it—no matter how hard I try, you're snotty, disrespectful and selfish. You wouldn't do your share if we were all bailing ourselves out of a sinking boat."

Mike: "Bad habit, Mom—sarcasm, shouting..." (Mom gives him a dirty look as his stopwatch goes beep.)

Susan: (interrupting) "Well, I've had it TOO. (Screaming) WORK, WORK, WORK is all I get! My friends have parents who LOVE them enough to give them TIME OFF. You're some kind of a sick, control freak!" (Susan goes into her room, showing by her body language that she hears the beep of Mom's stopwatch, and then she slams the door.)

Mom: (Clicks her stopwatch) "You're severely rebellious. You're on the clock, kid!"

Narrator: Mom forgot to take two deep breaths. Audience, she needs your help so she won't make things worse. Stretch and relax, Mom. Breathe deeply. Stretch again.

Mom: (Stopping herself from following Susan, she stretches and breathes deeply.) "Aw shi—shoot! Whatever I do isn't right."

Mike: (Stops his stopwatch with another "beep.") "Cheer up, Mom. Even God had trouble with Adam and Eve and they only had one rule!"

Mom: (Hugs him.) "You're right, sweetheart. And He was the perfect parent. I guess I'm ready to confess, take my medicine, and start over."

Mike: (Looking at his clipboard) "OK...Bad attitude attack for three minutes. Bad habit: minus four points for impulse problem. What is this, Mom, PMS or what?"

Mom: "Did you put down plus two for your healthy breakfast? And another plus two for impulse control...I felt like smacking her. Instead you can mark down plus eight, since I didn't use bad words and I restrained myself. When she comes out I'm going to negotiate a peace with her. I forgot she's in the monthly curse. Wait a minute...I'm there myself. My head hurts. My back hurts. I feel unloved." (Mom sits down by the kitchen table and sinks her head in her hands.)"

Mike: "Me too. Doug stole my dessert again today." (He sits down heavily into a chair.)

Susan: (Coming out of her room, crying) "I feel unloved, too!"

Mike: "Let's pray about it."

Mom: "You do it. I'm maxed out."

Mike: (Holding hands with Susan and Mom) "Lord, we got a mess here. Calm our mess down and help us to love. Amen."

Unison: After a pause, each looks at the others and says, "I love you guys/sweethearts."

Mom: "You ARE gifts from God. Help me to be a better Mom—especially around monthly curse time."

Susan: "You're O.K., Mom. Maybe we should keep it on the kitchen calendar. I'm sorry I lost my temper. Let's start over. I need a break from chores right now. I have a stomachache. May I just go lie down before dinner?"

Mom: "Yes, dear. Cool idea. Four points for a supportive solution. I'm going to lie down; too, for a half hour, and then we'll do chores. This could be a calcium/magnesium imbalance in us, Susan. Take two Cal-Mags and I will, too."

Dad: (Enters complaining while taking off his jacket.) "Hey, everybody, I'm home! What a rotten day. The CEO blamed me for what my boss failed to do and chewed me out. He'll probably put something in my personnel file. And I'm famished. Had to work through lunch hour...What's for dinner? (Noticing gloomy faces) Is something wrong?"

Mom: "I feel like a broken doll face down in a muddy ditch."

Dad: "What? Does your face hurt? Sinus infection?"

Narrator: "You have to spell it out for him, Mom. He thinks differently than you do."

Mom: (Buries her head in Dad's chest, mumbling) "Pray. Kids, fighting...PMS...don't feel loved."

Mike: "Good one, Mom. Plus four for impulse control again! You could have screamed. Plus another four on negotiation of a supportive solution...you and Susan are going to lie down for half an hour after taking chill pill minerals for your monthly curses."

Dad: "OOH! Is your weirdness catching? I'll drink some orange juice for a quick blood sugar fix so I won't get it. Mike, want to shoot a few hoops while the women get a grip?"

Mom: (Hugging Dad) "I love you. Mike, give Dad plus four for supportive solutions."

Mike: "Dad gets plus eight for two supportive solutions. I feel loved when we're shooting baskets."

Narrator: Notice that Susan still has negative points for rebellion. She will be held accountable for that. PMS is no excuse for poor behavior.

In brief: Lifelong love in a Christ-centered team provides satisfaction and security for parents and children. That kind of relationship is based on a balance of law and grace.

Understand the Strong-willed Child

Of course we cannot script our family life. Some parents will find their child testing them every day in every way for years. (Your reward is that these children are good thinkers.) Dr. James Dobson aptly discusses many variables in 🕮 *The Strong-Willed Child.*[35] If you are looking for a quiet, compliant child and a crisis-free life, get over it. You will not be happy with your child or your parenting until you modify your expectations to fit reality. I recall feeling that getting my strong-willed child to wear a safety belt took more effort than passing a bill through Congress.

Dr. Dobson's book has some essential tips on communicating with your strong-willed child. Do not be discouraged. It's tempting for a parent to change parenting techniques too soon, because "this one isn't working."

Do not worry. Stay with this system, even if all heaven doesn't break loose right away. You may have to wait years before a strong-willed child will "buy into" and cooperate completely with your system. Be assured, invisible progress is being made with God's help!

- ➥ Basics of this system were field-tested by Dr. Jones with every kind of child—average and difficult, emotionally disturbed, gifted, disabled, and delinquent, etc.—and he still found it to be the most effective system possible. Data show this approach outperforms the usual behavior modification and reinforcement techniques.[36]

Often troublemakers want meaning. This parenting system, based on sound research and eternal principles, is the best possible one long-term. Patience and endurance is essential to being a good parent! Be encouraged by this: My classroom experience convinces me that the "troublemakers" can be challenged and changed through giving them real responsibility in doing worthwhile tasks. Some of those power struggles are legitimate requests for more meaningful activity. Sometimes, the power struggles are caused by low self-esteem. Self-esteem is raised through taking a meaningful role in the group. Children get your positive attention, rather than stealing attention by negative choices.

Note: An interesting thing happens when angry or rebellious children pursue worthwhile tasks. In the process, children "buy into" the family system. Endorphins, brain chemicals that make us feel happy, are released. Endorphins are four hundred times more powerful than morphine. They not only give a sense of well-being but reduce pain. Think about it: interdependence is a legal high.

Section II

What You Must Know About Methods and Materials

View and Review the Expectations and Point Charts

Preview expectations with your spouse and your childcare provider. Discuss and prioritize problems. Do not tackle too much at once: This is a marathon, not a sprint. Absorb and discuss basics.

You will find that some close friends and relatives resist the changes you think are necessary. They prefer you to remain in the box they have designed for you. They prefer to stay inside their own comfort zone. Change is very uncomfortable, particularly if a person feels that you are criticizing the way he or she has always disciplined your children. Many issues will surface, and discussion may become heated. Be gentle but firm. Be complimentary. Get "ownership" of the process involved in learning and changing. Agree, in brief, on the goals and expectations. Then do a temporary three-month trial if you meet opposition.

When discussing authority issues, remember that the Parents' Point Chart and Expectations system not only helps you stay on target but also helps your child learn by vicarious experience. This is sneaky skill building at its best. You are not sitting your child down with a text and requiring structured memory work. Instead, you make an "assumptive close" to your sale of family values.

- ➥ When a child chooses to work with you or to go along with your agenda, he buys into your values without an immature debate over who's the boss.

Expectations 1 for Parents[37]

- Make breakfast, box lunches, dinner.
- Include 5-8 servings of fruit and vegetables for the day.

There. Was that tough? You choose the tasks you need reminders on. This is one example. Point Chart 1 for parents follows:

Parents' Point Chart 1

(Use this the second month of your program, keeping your child on Children's Point Chart 1)

– Negative Points		+ Positive Points	
1. Impulse problem (ignoring essential chores, health or safety)	- 2 each____	1. Impulse control – leadership ("I felt like ___, but instead I did this essential chore for our benefit" or following a plan)	+3 each ____ Grace Points +10 (Always start out with positive points – these are frace points)
Negative Points Total	- ________	Positive Points Total minus Negative Points Total Total Reward Points	________ ________ +/-________

Your child will need to have a ½ cup measure handy, for measuring the servings of cooked fruit or vegetable on your plate. One medium-sized piece of fruit counts for one serving. One half cup salsa or spaghetti sauce counts for one serving. A one cup measure will check the salad or raw vegetables available. That same knee-hugger-whiner who used to pinch his sister during dinner preparations will be busy dishing out food. He will make a mark for each time you fulfill a positive leadership role, such as making sure 5-8 servings of fruit or vegetables are available for the family each day. That's one mark. Add three more marks for breakfast, lunch, and dinner on the table.

Twelve marks mean twelve minutes playing an educational game with your child. Oops! Did you add grace points? That's 22 minutes in educational activity. You work too much anyway. Take a fun break. Try a math game. Have you ever used a Chinese abacus? It is a basic computer with beads. You can add, subtract, etc. There are basic math concepts involved in knowing, for example, that multiplication is a type of addition. It might be fun to check out a Chinatown near you, or go online for more information.

> Your child is learning math concepts, self-discipline, social skills, and conscientiousness. He is buying into your system without having rules laid on him.

After all, he is helping you, not memorizing under pressure. As you resolve your long-standing issues, children learn useful problem-solving behavior early. They thus avoid the vicious cycle of inheriting your faults, struggling with them, and passing them along to their children.

➥ This is not forcing children into adult roles since it is a voluntary process.

You are both submitting to God for guidance, and both relying on the Bible as your authority. The scope and sequence of your Parents' Charts is coordinated with your child's maturity level. As you begin Chart 2 with a child, use Parents' Point Chart 2 as soon as your child understands the concepts on it. Again, wait for your child to indicate she understands the vocabulary and can apply the ideas. Some children are very verbal, and others take a little longer. Do not judge or push your child over these parental issues. They can wait for the child's self-mastery. More detail on this comes later.

Take a look at the Children's Expectation Chart 1: You will gradually introduce all of these expectations, but begin with just one or two. Why?

- You have to train yourself to consistently enforce your expectations. Most parents only follow through half the time. You're better than average, or you would not have gone this far in the book! Go for the gold.

Keep it simple at first, but push for growth. Remember that your child must master—doing the chore fast and well—many adult skills by age eighteen, so do not slack off on your teaching. The sooner you include your child in the family team, the easier you will find introducing new skills. Teamwork and skill mastery are essentials of healthy adulthood.

Children's Expectations List 1

Free time starts when the chores are done.

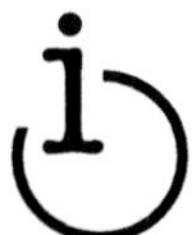

Remember the Scout Rule: If they are able to do it for themselves, do not do it for them.[38]

Basic chores (all under the Point Chart 1: Making a Mess or Cleaning Up category) for beginners. Begin when the child can talk well and understand basic directions. See text for teaching tips.

- Putting things away: Put pajamas away and dirty laundry into basket. Hang jackets on hooks. Put toys onto toy shelf. Keep schoolwork in sections.
- Empty his/her own trash basket and put it away again.
- Take his/her own dish to the table and then to the sink when finished eating.
- Brush teeth after meals.
- Stack or shelve magazines or books neatly in the child's area.
- Wash face and ears with soap and water.
- Dry up water spilled on bathroom floor with mop or big under-sink sponge.

The scoring system follows:

Children's Point Chart 1

– Negative Points		+ Positive Points	
Making A Mess (Spilling without wiping up, unmade bed, or leaving clothing, toys, etc., around while starting something else)	- 1 each___	**Cleaning Up** (Taking out trash, brushing teeth, carrying plates to sink, putting things away, helping others work.)	+2 each ___
Impulse Control Problem (Example: hitting, grabbing, insults, backtalk)	-2 each___	**Impulse Control and/or Teamwork** (Following directions or "I felt like ___, but instead I did this ___ for our benefit")	+3 each ___
Poor Breakfast or Late Breakfast, or Late Bedtime	- 1 each___	**Healthy Breakfast** On Time and/or In Bed On Time.	+2 each ___
Note: Outright Rebellion gets double consequences 1) Immediate down time or spanking and 2) Points off on the chart	-2 each specific instance	Always start out with positive points – these are Grace Points	Grace Points +10
Negative Points Total	______	Positive Points Total	______
		minus	
		Negative Points Total	______
		Total Reward Points	+/-______

Some of you parents are thinking, "Whew. That's better."

- ➥ Remember, do not hit your child with the whole list at once. These expectations are delivered to your child one at a time, according to the directions found later in this text.

Remember that rebellion receives double consequences: Immediate down time or spanking and points off on the chart. Down time may translate into minutes taken out of the end of a favorite TV show or into early bedtime.

Consider how you will review each expectation in detail with your child: Let him know he will do all the chores on the list when you decide he is able. Follow the Boy Scout Rule to decide when he is able. If he can physically perform the chore, he must do it by himself.

Begin with two or three chores and one to three rules of behavior (depending on the maturity of your child). One example of a behavior rule is this: "Keep your hands to yourself." Always avoid phrasing rules in the negative. A negative phrase would be "Don't touch what is not yours." According to Dr. Dennis Waitley, this kind of phrasing confuses the child. He cannot focus on the opposite of an idea. He then thinks, "Touch!" You are handicapped to start with if you use negative phrases.

Before you start the Children's Charts, make sure your expectations for "messes" points are posted and practiced. Practice several times, until you see the task become easier for your child. Begin with one or two problem messes, usually picking up toys or books, and food-related messes. Take the other chores for yourself until you judge that your child has mastered the first few.

Specific Detail: Once you have the general list of chores, reduce the generalities to specific tasks—on paper, using pictures for small children. Then be specific in walking through each chore with the child. For example, washing with soap and water should be done for 14 seconds, or the time it takes to sing one chorus of *Jesus Loves Me, This I Know!*

Walk through all chores in detail. First, you do it to demonstrate, making sure that you do not say more than three sentences of instruction to go along with your actions.

For chores that require more instruction than three simple sentences, break the chore into parts. Demonstrate first one part, and then the child does it without you while you observe in silence. If the child fails to meet your expectations, without expression say quietly, "No. Let's try again." Then you must repeat your actions and the same three simple sentences of instruction, and let your child do it without your input again. Next, demonstrate the second part of the chore and observe performance. Repeat this until the child can do each task completely and well.

A second way to give instruction involves partner learning. This method is used when you want complete, long-term memory and do not get it with the simpler technique above.[39]

With two children, or one child plus your spouse, demonstrate, then **write out instructions on a piece of paper or a flip chart**. Say the three simple sentences as you write them on the paper. Then learning partner #1 demonstrates, saying and writing the same three sentences. Next, the third person teaches partner #1 using the same demonstration, writing and saying the same three simple sentences.

Chore Time: Once the child proves to your satisfaction that she has mastered the task, follow through by having her do the same task daily. Remember that your child should not be begged, told twice or bribed to do this!

Announce that it is chore time. Then get in her face after making her stop what she is doing, look her in the eye, and speak the command specifically without any hint of a smile. Keeping your child on target is discussed in the boundaries section later.

Do not discourage your child by redoing his chore after he is finished. That says to the child that he is not a real team member, but a phony one. You will have to accept lesser quality while the child perfects his technique. Just remember to give lower points for lesser quality work.

Note: Practice is essential to success. Practice, practice, practice! Praise every step in the right direction. To make the process easier when you begin a new Expectations List, assign yourself a few of the harder chores by noting your initials to the side—then gradually ask your child to take over some of your "grown up" chores to allow all of you to have more fun time together.

Understand and Foster Maturity

Look for signs of maturity in yourself and your child: As your child slowly learns responsibility, you will see that your carefully structured teaching, prompts, and rewards for right behavior are working. Gradually your child will become strong enough to consistently make the right choices. Avoid all nagging, threats and punishing for routine issues, because this prevents your child from maturing. That is right! Do not retard your child in the name of kindness.

"Immature? Who, me?" By nagging, threats and punishment, you become responsible for starting correct behavior in the child.

She won't work without your nagging and threats. Your child then learns to be passive in the midst of things that need to be done. Remember that punishment is reserved for rebellion or safety issues.

When your child is passive in the midst of things that are to be done, this is actually passive aggression. Your child is rebelling, but feels unsafe and cannot be real with you.[40] There is no discipline if you have not created a safe communication environment. If you are busy criticizing, judging, dishonoring your child, denying his valid feelings, he will close his spirit against you. The control dramas you create then increase stress, destroy discipline, and become your legacy long after you are gone.

Your child needs your authoritative discipline without the added stress of negative emotional baggage. If you notice "tuned out" or "lazy" behavior, you have already reinforced learned helplessness and must train yourself and your child out of this cycle of immaturity.

When your parenting skills are primitive, your nagging and threats do not work. You immediately move into punishment mode because you slide down into the A-Zone. The adrenalin rush turns your brain into cotton candy. Repeat after me: "Skillful parenting is necessary for my sake as well as for my child. I have to learn this."

- ➥ When the issue is not safety or rebellion, spanking should be your final backup when all other techniques have failed. It will only be necessary on rare occasions (if ever) after the age of six.

Also, when you habitually stop a child from doing something by nagging, threats and punishment, your child learns to avoid censure and pain. You intimidate him unnecessarily. There will be times when you want your child to face and accept pain (especially social rejection) and censure (debate with unbelievers) without the added emotional burden of your negative conditioning. Childhood "tapes" will replay at the wrong times when you want your child to be bold. You want to free your child from subconscious emotional "brakes" which you may have installed by nagging, threats and heavy handed punishment. Instead we want discipline that is Stress-free as much as possible...not only for your sake but also for your child.

So what if I nag, threaten or punish to control my child's behavior? This is what happens. When you behave poorly, control for the child is always outside the child. This is a source of resentment, anger, and frustration. Your external control becomes something the child will resist by counterforce, lies or other maneuvers in order to win the power struggle.

The instant your child leaves home (or enters the classroom), she will "rebel" against the authority she sees as a threat to her pride, power, and self-esteem. Self-control, then, does not develop until the child runs into other, more drastic reinforcers such as the principal, courts, police, and firing policy at work. "Moral maturity," according to Dr. Jones, is thus "arrested at an early childhood level."[41]

There is another possibility: Your child may become a compliant, dependent dupe, accepting your excessive external control by becoming totally dependent...unable to think for himself. This child is the perfect victim for Bible-based cults or predators.

How does too much punishment sabotage good discipline? Good discipline is internal after you have built self-control into your child. You do not have to be there to have your child behave well. Personal respect and caring between you and your child joins you into a team, where everybody is motivated to follow the rules for living.

Punishment is your last resort discipline measure, but many parents do not know what to do besides punishment. Know this: Punishment is not only stressful (meaning upset and burnout for you), but also causes alienation (distance) and rejection in your child's world. Alienation destroys relationship. It makes huge withdrawals from your love bank...the one you have been making deposits in as your child grows.

You get obedience and cooperation when you are careful not to empty your child's love bank. A useful book in this regard is 🕮 *The Five Love Languages* by Gary Chapman, Northfield Publishing. As Dr. Jones says "Relationship is by far the most effective and efficient form of behavioral management."[42]

Every bit of praise, each hug, all those shared victories and joys make deposits in your child's love bank. Every punishment destroys your team spirit, sometimes even the child's motive to do what's right and good. Punishment separates you from your child, and destroys his motivation to cooperate. With alienation and no cooperation, where is the team? While punishment is necessary and biblical, it is not the only option. Spanking, for example, should only be used in situations of rebellion or danger. Keep reading to find what to do besides punish. There are many steps before this last one.

Internal Freedom: When you nurture your child into maturity, he has an entirely different idea of freedom. When he enters the demanding world of fifth or sixth grade, he is able to successfully govern his own behavior. He already has an internal set of controls and values that you have gradually built.

Freedom becomes the ability to make right choices without being forced or entering conflict. Being competent, your child does not have to prove himself. He likes himself and finds acceptance in doing the right thing.

At the same time, you do not want to push your child into maturity when he clearly is not able. Young girls mature faster than boys do. Look for signs of stress to decide whether you are pushing too fast or requiring too much. Most signs of stress involve sleep or eating disturbances. Sudden illness when facing a test at school is another sign of stress. Try to pinpoint what brings on the stomachache or other illness. Never reward this type of illness with excess sympathy, gifts, fun or games. If the child stays home from school, it should be terribly boring for him. Ask your pediatrician for his guidelines on stress in children.

If your child cries too easily or too fast, consider whether this is the well-used game children use to get their way. Watch how long your emotional child can focus on television or other fun activities, as opposed to how long she can stay on task with chores. Do not be fooled by emotional ploys, but take personality differences into account. This is another use you may make of the Personality Analysis I have included in the Appendix.

In short: We must be serious students of our children. We must know their love language, their feelings, their attention span, their personality and thinking style, their maturity, their needs. If we cannot "read" our children, we're running a hotel, not a home.

Set Your Family Up for Success

Add Perks and Sleep

When you add harder chores to your child's area of responsibility, consider adding slightly more "perks," such as going to bed 10 minutes later at night because he "is taking on more adult responsibilities." If you have not required a specific bedtime for your child, do it now. Make it early.

A Harvard sleep study determined years ago that peak performance at school and at home required the average child (through age 18) to get nine hours of sleep nightly. Dr. William C. Dement, M.D., considers sleep debt a national emergency. He says children and teens need an average of about ten hours. Sleep deprivation causes many fatal traffic accidents due to "micro-sleeps." Further, we are poor judges of how rested we really are.[43] Parents, do not listen when your teen argues with you on this.

Limit Stimulation

Children need a calming down period before bedtime. TV and video games are not relaxing. A bath is relaxing, then some personal sharing time. A proverb is a good thing at this time, since there are just enough chapters in Proverbs to use the date as a study guide. You can read chapter 1 on the first day of the month, Proverbs 2 on the second, etc. The object of our focus just before bedtime is rehearsed in our sleep.

You will need to deprive your teenager of TV or computer in the bedroom, if you want to make sleeping rules stick. Also, avoid outside jobs for teens until all family needs are met. Usually, once a teen gets a car, grades go down and sleeping patterns become erratic. Keep in close touch with teachers. Feedback once weekly is a good idea for any child who shows tendencies toward disorganization. As a parent, it is your responsibility to make sure distractions do not destroy your family unity and teamwork. Make your family, your child's health and education the priorities regardless of the various tactics your teen will use to get his or her way.

You will also need to deprive yourself—of stressful, fragmenting, focus-destroying influences. Dr. Archibald Hart has written several books and articles around this subject. We have become addicted to the adrenalin rush of our over-stimulated culture to our detriment. This addiction wears out our body and our minds. Frankly, we think in sound bytes because we have conditioned ourselves to self-distract with various media. Stop it now.

> I believe we have trained ourselves to skim the surface of serious thinking, just like the Bible predicted. (We cannot endure sound doctrine; we want fast wisdom and entertainment.) If God had wanted sound-byte thinking, He would have put the Bible on a DVD.

Therefore, I suggest you avoid over-stimulating video games, arguments when you are tired, and other mental "flak"—especially just before bedtime. Those things only get rehearsed in your sleep.

Remember Philippians 4:6-8. Solitude and quiet time with God's Word are essential "soul food." Are you starving yourself?

A victory journal is a great stress buster. If you keep a praise or victory journal, you will find yourself very encouraged at what you and God have done as a team. You will not have to write every day, but a weekly review of what you have written serves as worship as well as stress-busting encouragement. Check out your old charts and the progress you have made. Share with your learning partner. Uplift each other. Every step in the right direction is reason to celebrate.

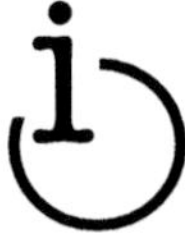

In short: Grandma was right. Get enough rest, exercise and fresh air, and avoid biting off more than you can chew. Also remember Philippians 4:6-8.

Build Team Spirit

Whenever changes are made, get ownership if you can. That means your child should take part in creating the new deal if possible. Without this, you may not get cooperation. You may get rebellion when your back is turned, especially at first.

Create the expectations with your child's help if the child will cooperate. Don't give open-ended choices. However, if your child is strong-willed and uncooperative, give a choice between two specifics: "You may choose to (1) rinse and wash or (2) dry and put away dishes. Which chore do you want?"

Democratic management is the best option when children are receptive. To begin, say, "Let's think of some ways you and I can help each other so we will both have more time for fun. I feel grouchy when I don't have time for fun, don't you? Let's write down all my chores, along with how long each one takes." You may use our Expectations List for parents (which follows) or create your own list.

One time study found that grocery shopping, meal planning and preparation, set-up, and clean-up requires twenty hours of effort per week for a family with two children (without the extra work of homemade recipes). Realize that we usually underestimate the time something takes by about 30 percent, so add that to your first guess as to how long each chore takes.

Appeal to the child's sense of fairness when he sees your long list of chores. Then create the list of chores for your child.[44] Up to age 8, children may need or prefer pictures cut from magazines as well as a sentence cue on their chore charts.

If your child is so used to having his or her own way that he refuses to create a chart with you, you'll need to start with basics, and make one without his or her input.[45] Even God has trouble with people.

Make it clear that grown-ups usually have to do their chores before they can have fun, and you're teaching the child to be grown up. Your child needs to be aware that being grown up involves freedom with responsibility. Later you can teach how to prioritize chores, so the essential ones—high priorities—get done first.[46] If you hear a big groan and see eyes rolling toward the ceiling, explain how positive helping the family really is. Grownups can get high on doing worthwhile tasks. Yes! Endorphins—brain chemicals—reduce fatigue and increase our joy.

➥ **Explaining the RAS Dynamic:** At the base of our skull, just above the spine, there is a small part of our brains called the Reticular Activating System (RAS). This small bit of gray matter coordinates both sides of our brain like an autopilot coordinates parts of an airplane engine. It makes sure the job is done whenever we make a conscious decision.

The RAS works for both positive and negative goals. That is why parents must be especially careful to control their tongues. Since every idle (fruitless) word is recorded in heaven, and you will be called to account for yourself to God, pray right now that you do not program your child with negative remarks. Christians ought never to say things like, "You'll never learn." Notice your negative thoughts and kill them before they multiply.

Here's an example: If we decide we cannot dance, the RAS makes sure we are truly clumsy. If we decide that we will hate, loath and detest helping out with family chores, we will find ourselves in great pain while doing family chores. We choose how we will feel!

Any conscious decision is reinforced with action via the RAS. This is why we do not allow our hysterical little girl to get away with not doing her chores when she cries. She will remember if that trick works. Make sure she has consequences for disobedience. Allow her time to sit quietly by herself, with no toys, until she decides to work. Put her in the playpen if she is young enough.

Even if your child cannot yet speak English, she understands a great deal more than you think. A two-year-old may have a vocabulary anywhere from 12 to 1,000 words. I.Q. is measured primarily in the number of words a person has mastered. Words are ideas. If your child has a high vocabulary, she will be better able to understand and cope with her world.

If you choose to teach your child sign language you will find that he not only grasps concepts early, but can communicate with you about them. By the way, if you teach your child sign language, you will increase his IQ by 10 points before he even begins to speak. His ability to communicate will decrease his tantrums (frustration) and your stress. Seven dollar flashcard sets for teaching children are available online.

When we choose to do our best at a worthwhile job, our brain automatically helps us to carry it through. Not only are the right and left sides of the brain coordinated (they are often on different "tracks") but we also produce the endorphins that energize and encourage us. We are cheerful and feel no pain, even when we are doing strenuous work.

Ask for help: When you decide on chores, begin by saying to your child that you need his/her help. A toddler can—and should—take his dirty diaper to the trash or diaper pail, and can even wash out the hard stuff in the toilet before putting a diaper in the pail. The child can then wash his hands with soap and warm water. You will have to literally walk him through this process over and over until he does it on his own. Toddlers are very concrete, physical little people. Rewards on the Point Chart should be reviewed daily for the small child, weekly for those who are able to defer gratification (delay rewards).

In short: Democratic management within limits that you set is a good way to build up your children. Our body chemistry is designed to support worthwhile family activities.

Set (Do Not Destroy) Boundaries with Your Body Language

Setting boundaries is an essential skill which requires practice. Set yourself up for success by practicing your boundary-setting with your spouse or learning partner—or at least before the mirror. Ten or fifteen minutes are not enough for this. Imagine yourself in your most recent failure at discipline, and rerun your actions to express power and confidence.

Here's why: Body language tells your child whether you mean what you have said or not. A smile during discipline says you do not mean what you are saying. It is a signal among primates that they are submitting to the dominant primate! A smile at this time—when you're giving a command—says you are begging or submitting to the child. Practice in front of a mirror until you get it right. Open-handed, apologetic body language will not get you the results you need. Have a friend video you with your child so you can read your own body language.

> Unsuccessful decoys only make you think you are delivering discipline. The worst of these is nagging and posturing without doing anything. Your children must know from your body language that you have all day to enforce the rules. You must be calm, be close, and take time in the beginning. This is the "meaning it" stance which causes bad behavior (and time spent in discipline) to disappear over time.[47]

When the words and the gestures do not agree, the child will read your gestures. If your child does as he or she wants, he has decided from your body language that you either don't mean it or you won't make the consequences at all tough. Remember how you couldn't get away with breaking rules in Miss Mean's third grade class? Realize that "nice" doesn't "mean it" when maturity is being required of your child. Growth into rule-following behavior and interdependence is never comfortable. Children rarely volunteer for this assignment.

If your child is a youth or teenager, the process is the same as above. When you give specific directions in the manner I suggest, you should not have to repeat them, explain them or negotiate them. If your teen is used to getting her way by manipulating you, this will become a battle of wills. Ignore whatever the child says to get your goat. This takes practice. Role play this proactive—non-reactive stance with a friend or in front of a video camera or mirror.

For those of us who were raised to "be nice," confrontation like this is extremely difficult. Let's face it, your children have raised you from their childhood. They know what buttons to push in order to get their way with you. The charmer and the negotiator are no less disobedient than the child who strides forth to take control. Remind yourself that the easy road leads downhill.

My best lessons on parent power came from my Grandma Goldie and Dr. Frederic Jones. When I was a child, Grandma Goldie's discipline had all the grace and finality of a Sherman tank. I could not fool her or escape the consequences of my poor choices. As I write this, I am not sure where Grandma Goldie leaves off and Dr. Jones begins. However, Dr. Jones puts it best: "Any time you want to increase your power,

Shut up,
slow down,
relax,
get close, and
kill time."[48]

Practice steps 1-5. Stay silent. Slow down with deep breathing. Relax your shoulders and stomach. Get within three feet of your child. Move slowly closer if the bad behavior continues after you are close. Get eye to eye and stay there while your child squirms and tries to make you go away.

When more that one child is misbehaving, focus your attention on the child who appears to be the worst offender. Remember that the child who gives you the charming smile may be the worst "underhanded" rebel—the one who plans the mischief and gets a brother or sister to look guilty.

> ➥ While you relax, get close and remain silent, Dr. Jones suggests you kill time. I suggest you spend time praying, so you get God working on your specifics and get your mind off the confrontation. You can't walk on water. Peter sank when he looked at the angry waves rather than at Jesus. Your breathing will be the first thing you forget, the most difficult skill to master.[49]

Your prayer might be something like, "Lord, calm my spirit. Give me right judgment. Conform Your children to Your will. Fix this mess. Amen."

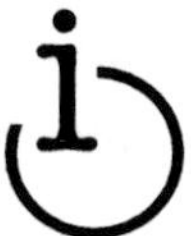

In short: Memorize the above five steps to personal power. Then practice, practice, practice.

Prevent Misbehavior By Moving in Close

Why move close? We want the cost of enforcing rules to be cheap: We do not want to be making unnecessary withdrawals from our child's love bank. That is why you cannot afford to become upset or to be distant. Yet you must get good results. Yelling from the next room is not going to get the results you want. It will teach your child that you do not mean what you say.

Prevent small disruptions by perpetual motion: invisible discipline. Children may complain that you are always there, but it will stop misbehavior in the bud. You will be seeing some of those secret misbehaviors when children are tripping baby brother or inciting violence. They can then be separated or distracted from brawls. One technique is to assign chores to the sly saboteur. Put him in the room where you are working.

Some of the petty behavior which grows into bigger problems is based on a need for attention. Positive attention is better than the negative attention of punishment, but a child who needs attention will get any kind of attention rather than go without. *Stress-free Discipline* provides the attention children need, both positive and negative.

We need to keep rules being followed with a sense of calm and love and cooperation. As time passes, your control will appear effortless, but children will behave well. The way should always be open for personal choice and—as necessary—for reconciliation. Isn't that what Jesus would do?

In short: Good discipline will eliminate 80 to 90 percent of the disobedience, disruption and stress which occurs in your home. It is important to look in on children often. Your mobility often prevents any need for punishment.

Practice Moving in Techniques to Set Yourself Up for Success

Keep your eyes and ears open

Much as you might like to forget your duties as parent, you must be constantly monitoring your child's behavior. That is why their play places should be close to your work station.

Dinnertime seems to be the worst time. Fussy, fighting children are either hanging on to your knees or pinching each other. Knowing this, you can prepare most of dinner in the morning (or on the weekend) when the children (and you) are most likely to be feeling rested. At that time they are most likely to be playing peacefully without your input. Then, think of some food-related chores for them to do at the dinner hour—five-year-olds can set the table. If necessary, hire a neighbor teenager to play with them for an hour or two while you do your chores.

Just remember to be alert. If you fail to be aware, you are inviting your child to gamble that you will not see his misbehavior or do anything about it.

Stop what you are doing as soon as you sense misbehavior. Face the problem child and give her "the look." No smiles, no frown, no "pretty please" body language, no talk. Keep your hands quietly below your waist or behind your back. If you are with one child while another one misbehaves, excuse yourself from what you are doing with the first child. If you happen to be teaching, reading to the child, or other special activities, realize that discipline comes before everything else. The reason is that nothing else can take place without basic order and respect.

Discipline comes where? Before everything else.

Face the offender, look, say the child's name, and chill out. Relax, take deep breaths, and see what your offender will do. Pray. This sounds simple, but there are many ways you can do this step wrong, usually by moving too fast. If you fail here, you will be pushed into using stronger discipline methods. Stronger methods will escalate the conflict and cost you more time and more peace of mind.

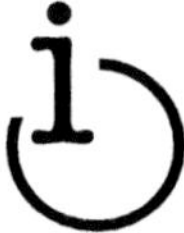

In short: The moving in and moving out sequences are essential to your successful discipline. Practice these techniques to avoid more stressful escalation of the conflict.

Master Crucial Skills: Practice, Practice, Practice

Nine crucial skills, those most difficult to master and most easily forgotten follow. Study and practice these methods. Practice, practice, practice. Stop. Begin deep breathing to avoid adrenalin-driven brain fog.[50]

1. Turn around completely from what you are doing.
2. Face the offender squarely. (Partial turns tell your child you are not committed to dealing with her.)
3. Look her in the eye. Take two deep breaths: slow everything by 15 seconds. (Poor or furtive eye contact shows lack of confidence. Children will also read your eyes if they are wide. That means you are upset and the child is in control. An aggressive teen will interpret your wandering

eyes as discomfort and anxiety. He will decide that you will not stay in this situation or follow through.)

4. Keep your face expressionless...totally relaxed. (A smile or frown shows fear, anxiety, and anger. A child can read your set jaw across the room. Your child is in control of you whenever you cannot control yourself.)
5. Do not smile back if he or she smiles at you. (Smiling even a little or laughing in a stressful moment says you are submitting—giving up the competition.) Relax and wait.
6. Keep your hands below your waist, hanging comfortably (not on your hips or folded). To prevent nervous mannerisms with your hands, place them behind your back.
7. Say the name only once, loudly enough to be heard, with a bland or flat tone.
8. Relax with two more deep breaths. If you are ever in doubt about what to do next, take two more deep breaths. This is slow motion.
9. Read your child's body language. If it says, "I submit" early in the above sequence, you do not need to go further. You just want to calm things down. However, there is a phony compliance which you need to understand. That is in the next section.

In brief: Grandma was again right. Discipline comes before everything else. We must discipline ourselves before we can discipline our children. Visualize your latest discipline failure and rerun it as a success. Imagine yourself doing all of the eight steps without a hint of a smile, or other submissive body language. Study and practice the above eight steps at least twenty times in front of a mirror or with your learning partner.

- Pay the price of success up-front, or pay a higher price in constant power struggles for many years. Prevention is always cheaper than patch, fix, patch, and patch.

Understand Your Child's Body Language

Fake Out

If your child gives you the "I submit" smile, do not take this as true compliance until you check his "lower half." When your child still has his body partly turned toward his baby brother, whom he has been teasing, your child is escalating the conflict but hopes you will fold and go away. This body language means he is committed to doing things his way.[51]

You must persuade him that he cannot win this game. You must continue with moving close and the eight steps listed before. Relax but do not move back. If conflict continues, plant yourself between the two children, with your eyes remaining on the worst offender. You have now moved within the personal comfort zone of your child with your unsmiling, neutral face.

- By now you are asking yourself, "Do I have to spend so much time?"

Have courage, Mom. If you turn back to making dinner, you just lost the game. Poor behavior will continue. Remember, nagging and threats are not appropriate at this time. Do not strut or posture like a rooster; your children know the strut means nothing.

Punishment does not need to occur at this time, either. I remember getting spanked for "doing nothing—now do something and see what you get." Clearly my smiling face did not impress my mother. Charm should not impress you either. Your consistent consequences will make spanking less and less necessary.

However, do not worry about creating a violent child when spanking is necessary. Safety and intelligent obedience are essential survival skills your child must master. There are no well designed scientific studies which confirm the idea that spanking by a loving parent breeds violence in children.

Keep yourself in top shape, just like a marathon runner. You will be more alert, effective and loving. Energy drain caused by overwork, poor breathing, insufficient rest or poor nutrition drives love out of your relationships.[52] Take care to prevent these. Your body is a temple to God. Take care of it.

The next step: If your troublemaking child shows cooperation by being turned completely toward you or to an appropriate activity, you can begin moving out of the scene. This also must be done properly, or you will sabotage all your discipline to this point.

If you have two children who are troublesome, you will need to move your attention and your body to the second child, facing that child squarely. Then you will look him in the eye, with completely relaxed face, and shoulders relaxed while you breathe slowly.

Meaning it: Your time spent watching the children is seen by them as commitment and follow-through. When they decide you "mean it" your children are more likely to cooperate. You're the leader. Act it out.

When the second child turns completely toward you, away from the rivalry with his brother, you will wait, breathe, and then thank the child after he resumes his chore or his play in an appropriate manner.

Practice Your Moving Away Technique

Step 1: Thank your cooperative child and wait another two slow breaths (15 seconds). This is long enough for you to watch you child's behavior.[53]

Step 2: If it is all right, you may walk away slowly. Remember, if you move too fast your body language says you are uncomfortable. The child has won if you are not in control of yourself. Before leaving the room completely, turn slowly and look again. If all is well, resume what you have been doing.

Confront Continual Misbehavior

Here's the Problem

Suppose you have heard a disruption, stopped in your tracks, turned to face the child completely, given the "look," and said the child's name. You have moved to within three feet of the child and waited (relaxed and watching). The children are continuing their misbehavior. You have approached the more aggressive of the two and the child has not moved. This artful disrespect says, "So what?" She is escalating the conflict. This puts the ball in your court.

The Prompt

Your next step is a prompt. This is a clear, short neutral message telling your child precisely what to do next. It may be a verbal or a physical prompt. No blame, no debate, no sarcasm, remembering to breathe, you move with deliberate grace. Mom, you are the queen mother, your child is only the princess.

You may move another toy in front of the child, open a book, or take away some disputed item.[54] Ignoring complaints, you look with extreme boredom at the offender. Do not roughly push the child, since this often angers a disobedient person, especially teens. You do not want to make things worse. A toddler may need to be physically redirected with "No!" spoken firmly, but if his attention span is good he may return to pulling the dog's ears or other "No-no." On the second offense (or obvious movement toward that goal), distract him or remove him to a barren playpen for a few minutes.

Keep it Simple

One or two simple sentences will tell the child what to do next. Tell the child to begin work on a specific task.

You might say something like this:

- Read a book quietly or help me in the kitchen. What do you choose?
- Find another toy or take a time-out. Which is it?
- Show me your homework. It is time to begin.
- No homework? You need to practice your penmanship. Bring me paper and pencil and the dictionary.

Remember Grandma Goldie: There is no excuse for disobedience. Delay is disobedience.

Take No Prisoners, Accept No Compromise

After you give the prompt, do not retreat. Stay close and take two deep breaths ("belly breathing, shoulders down). If you have trouble with this, count "one thousand one, one thousand two," until you get to "one thousand fifteen."

Remain in the child's face until you get compliant body language—getting back on some task—and respectful sentences. Then thank your child after you have taken two breaths, and stop your moving in process with the worst troublemaker. Quietly mark negative points for disrespectful talk (insults, putdowns or profanity, blaming or sarcasm) under impulse control on the chart. Before you mark a child down for these (see the next section) you will have identified them all and given examples for each one.

Make sure your child knows precisely what is an insult, put down, etc.

Next, move your attention to the second child, and give her equal time. After you have watched her get back to peaceful activity, thank her and begin moving away slowly after marking negative points for any disrespectful talk.

Do not tell your child that his body language has tipped you off, or he will use it to lie to you in the future.

Do Not Give Major Instruction at This Time

If your child asks you how to do something and you can be distracted from your discipline process, that tactic will be used on you for the rest of his childhood. Tell him, for example, to begin handwriting practice without you and you will attend to his question later.

Your child will probably feel that the price of attracting your unfavorable attention is too high to keep it up. He will play or read quietly. If not, you are dealing with back talk.

In short: Setting boundaries with body language looks like it takes too much time for busy parents. It does take time at first. However, when it is done properly, time-consuming discipline disappears as behavior improves. Remember to give equal time to all troublemakers, the schemer and the follower. This tells them you are confident (be calm), committed (take time), and intense (get close).

Ignore All Back Talk But Take Off Points

Your child will have several possible reactions to having you close and focused. One is back talk, which may include anything from a joke, a compliment, and insults to a profane attack. Your child wants you gone, and has practiced the art of getting rid of you well enough to know what tactic has worked before.

You are not to engage in debate or wit or the game of "Top this!" which your child will try to carry on. That is so difficult for us. However, children are masters in the game of verbal provocation.

> ➥ It is so tempting to talk away your stress. Bite your tongue.

There are several types of back talk. Back talk is any non-compliant speech or behavior. These include making faces, helplessness, denial, blaming, accusing, excusing, insults and profanity.[55] All back talk has the same goal, whether it is confrontational or not. The goal is parent control. Dr. Jones teaches in detail about back talk. When you are ready for in-depth work I again recommend that you take his workshops.

Back talk may not be aggressive; it might be a defense mechanism. It might be simple imitation of something your child has seen in other families or on TV. See if you can sense the emotion behind the talk.

> ➥ Verbal aggression is the most common weapon used in social situations. "Insults" come from a Latin word meaning "to leap upon." Some people use taunts that are hurtful because of their sarcasm, irony or tone of voice. "Put-downs" call attention to a parent's faults or mistakes or weaknesses. These put-downs are used to humiliate another person.

Another form of verbal aggression is profanity. People who use profanity when they want to make their point forcefully are really using it to help themselves manipulate or dominate another.

Blaming is usually an application of our "shoulds" or "oughts" to another person. This usually escalates aggression, even if it is true.

Most of the time, it is the fault of both people in an argument. It takes two to tangle. Remember how Eve blamed the snake and Adam blamed God for giving him Eve?

Verbal aggression is one step toward conflict, and needs to be carefully identified for your child when you are not both in the midst of conflict. Wait until a quiet time when nobody is in the "A-Zone" for any reason. Then talk through definitions and examples of each of the above, to clarify for your child what she is doing.

In short: Do not react to back talk or disrespect, but hold a child accountable for it by negative marks on the chart. One negative mark per incident is enough. The next back talk of an incident gets another mark.

Perhaps the greatest "sucker play" a child uses in the midst of discipline is helplessness. If you fall for it, your agenda—obedience—is gone. Poof! Suppose your children have been told to pick up their toys before dinner, but they are pushing each other instead. Your child will say something like "I'll clean up the playroom if you'll just show me how," or "I can't. I need help." You have already walked through chores in detail. Now, if you fall for it, your child just got away with defiance. She is writing a master's thesis on parent control.

➥ Never mix instruction with discipline.[56]

Instead, look with utter boredom at your helpless child and wait. After fifteen seconds, if you feel you must say something, say "Try" or say, "Do what you can. I'll help you later." Then you can move on to giving equal time to your other child who cannot be allowed to think he is exempt from your withering attention. Play deaf to their comments.

Another misunderstood form of back talk is excusing you to leave. It may take several forms:

"O.K., I'll do it."

"O.K., I'll do it if you just leave me alone."

"O.K. Quit bugging me. Go away. I'll do it!"

Again, you look with utter boredom at your defiant child and wait. After fifteen seconds, if you feel you must say something, say "Now."

Insults usually focus on your body or your personality. Practice ignoring these with your learning partner.

- Remember, you look with utter boredom at your defiant child and wait. Say nothing. You are underwhelmed.

Profanity will completely upset most parents and completely distract them from the discipline process. Again, you look with utter boredom at your defiant child and wait. Say nothing. Breathe. Pray.

Later you will record the word with negative points under "impulse control," but now is not the time. Simply count the number of times a child uses profanity. Use your fingers behind your back if you sense you are getting emotional and forgetful. Maintain eye contact. Wandering eyes say you do not mean to follow through.

Other efforts to get you off track (and your child off the hook) include crying, compliments, changing the subject, pushing you aside, or hugs and kisses. Do nothing. Nada. Nothing. Wait until the child has returned to picking up the toys, or until he responds to your prompt with his body language. Never give in. Never give up on the discipline process. You will often get an apology for back talk. Feel free to reward the apology with a forgiving hug. Negative points are still awarded. Going through a red light still earns a ticket.

There is no substitute for the self-esteem earned through service. If you think—perhaps subconsciously—that the parent exists to serve the child, get over it. Biblically, the child is judged by what he can do, but he is judged. You must teach him to be obedient, serving his own family, before he will care about being useful to society. If he receives praise for being useful to you, he will want to have praise for good works from others.

In brief: Any form of non-compliance is back talk. Keep up the sequence of setting boundaries until you see by your child's body language that he is on task. Hold him accountable for verbal aggression by points off his chart under impulse control. He has the right to disagree, but must learn not to be disagreeable.

Master the Follow-up Sequence

Ping Time

Ping time works like this. Suppose your child has not responded to your close attention and prompt. This is full blown rebellion, but you have one more step before you spank him. You must "ping" him by starting your stopwatch. You will record the length of time he chooses to disobey. You have been prepared for this by wearing a watch with stopwatch feature or a regular stopwatch handy around your neck. Your clipboard is close at hand.[57] Ping again when the child begins to do what you asked. *Record the ping time on your chart.* Then impose down time or spanking as you see fit. The down time may be taken off of the favorite TV program or other cherished activity if it occurs on the same day as the offense. Down time will come into your discipline picture more and more as a preschooler becomes more verbal and grows up. Spanking, as discussed elsewhere, is primarily for children under six.

Suppose you impose spanking or down time after your child begins to do what he was asked. Your child will complain that he is now doing as he was asked. "It's not fair!!" You counter with: Even though a speeder slows down, he must still pay the fine for speeding.

You have two options:

- If your child is immature (or strong-willed) and has continued in disobedience, keep the stopwatch going. Then ground the child on the floor or into a chair, spanking if he moves off his seat. When he is quiet in his seat, stop your timer and do the follow-up below.
- If your child is more compliant, beginning to do what is expected of him, stop and record ping time and then follow up.

The Follow-Up

Take two deep breaths! Then sit down (preferably with the child) with your clipboard and a piece of scratch paper, (kept at the back). Note the command not followed. Also write a negative impulse control mark on your clipboard. Say nothing until you score the behavior. Keep up the deep breathing.

If your child hastens to obey, he will only have a few seconds recorded in the "rebellion" section of his chart. These points may be totaled up for the day, and grounding done in the evening. If the child continues to disobey after getting negative points and down time, start the stopwatch again. When he is on task, end the ping time and impose more down time.

Finally, when it's over, he may still be in the "A-Zone" where adrenalin plays hardball with his brain. He may have forgotten the original command. In that case, draw his attention to the scratch paper, writing the command while you are saying it. Then say, "Do it now." If the child then obeys, record positive points for doing the chore.

Never award full points for a quality job if the child had to be told twice to do it. Your written command will remind the child (when tallying up points time comes) that he or she had to be told twice.

If he takes off out the door, he may have to be physically brought back and "grounded" instantly. That means he must sit in the corner, or in an empty, boring place without toys or books. He stays there for the amount of time he was in rebellion. Another effective grounding time occurs during his favorite television program.

Gentle Persuasion

Some children will have to be grounded in a chair near you if they struggle to stay in a corner away from your work site. At this point, your only other option is a spanking and a change of place for down time.

If he jumps off the chair, he gets a good spanking. It is memorable. Not a light swat. It must bring genuine tears, and you will sense the difference. Judicious spanking is sometimes necessary. However, some strong-willed children seem to thrive on punishment. That is why you will want to set up a series of back-up tactics which we will discuss as we move on.

Be aware of the rules for and definitions of child abuse in your state. In California, spanking is considered child abuse and Child Protective Services can remove your child from your home. Always make sure your child understands how necessary it is to listen and obey rules. Make sure the rules are clear. Have your child repeat the rule that he or she broke back to you before you give a spanking.

Talk about traffic rules. They are there to prevent hurt. Make an appointment to take your child down to the police station and show him or her the jail. Have a policeman or woman talk about rules for safety. Talk about traffic lights: stop means stop. Never run a red light or you are a bad example.

A hug and "I love you too much to let you disobey" are good after you write the negative points and ground and/or spank the child. If the disobedience is a bid for loving attention, you'll see that by the child's reaction: he'll obey you without further ado. You have not caused an emotional scene, leaving a poison residue which will cause underhanded anger and further disobedience. You have not shouted at your child, tripping into the A-Zone and making things worse.

Obedience at this point does not mean the child gets out of being grounded. The child also still gets the negative points. And yes, this is double punishment. Rebellion must have strong consequences. The price must be high enough to convince your child that rebellion is not worth it.

"Free time" for the child is not free until your child habitually obeys you.[58] Let the child know that obedience is his ticket to free time. "Doing his own thing" instead of teamwork within the family must never get rewarded with free time. Remember, no talk, just the beep of the stopwatch and the sound of you recording points.

Team Points for Added Incentives

If you have several children, you may award points to teams or to the whole flock. If you have three children, you might team up the oldest child with baby and Daddy with the middle child, then later team up Mommy with baby and the oldest with your middle child. Team management means that one score sheet is used to give points to two or more children.

➥ Team management should solve some sibling rivalry problems.

It would be fun to have team colors and a motto or even a song. Make of it what you will. Ecclesiastes 5:18 entitles us to enjoy our labor as a gift from God, if I read it right. Work, then, ought to be fun if we can make it so.

It is the task of the team to decide which expectations should be the responsibility of what person on the team. You may want to list each chore on a 3 x 5" card, with your guess as to how much time it will take, so the chores may be kept handy in a pocket.

Suppose you have chosen to team up an oldest and youngest child in team A, while the two middle children are team B. Parents will decide what Expectations Charts to use in order to have the jobs be fairly evenly matched in time and effort. Parents may wish to assign chores if the team cannot make assignments without parents.

It will be natural that some children are more socially mature or more focused and willing to work. "To whom much is given, much is required" was a phrase used often around our house.[59] A bright, high energy person with leadership potential needs to develop the qualities of leadership. You will want to read and discuss Nehemiah's approach to leadership.

It is very possible to require less of a small child (in order to earn top points) than of a teenager to earn the same points. Praise liberally, but realistically. Always reward the child for every step toward competence, but do not pile on the work out of proportion.

We need to be sensitive to the point at which challenge becomes excessive, overwhelming a child and bruising the fruit. This needs to be as fair and as fun as possible.

Your mellow youngest child may be more comfortable in a negotiator role. Each person is respected and rewarded for his or her giftedness.

You want the goals to be doable. You want to inspire rather than to require challenging performance. You are the coach; your children are the team. You challenge them to communicate with diplomacy, speaking the truth in love. It is challenging to learn a new skill. Often a younger child will welcome learning skills from an older sibling rather than directly from you. The older sibling will enjoy getting credit for mentoring the little pest. That credit would come under impulse control or win/win negotiation.

You will want to be sure no undue force is used by an older child on a younger one. Also make sure the older child does not "just do" the younger person's chores himself. This means points off, after explaining what "tough love" is.

> Tough love allows a person to struggle in order to grow. Cheating in the growth process will stunt one's growth.

A butterfly is an example children can understand. The chrysalis must be painfully pushed open at the right time and it is a struggle. Without that struggle, the butterfly is not mature enough to fly. If the chrysalis is cut open to allow an easy exit, the butterfly has no strength to function. It cannot fly and is easy prey to birds.

- Trees show the same need for "tough love." Roots go deep when the wind is strong, growing strength to match the stress. A tree with no opposition will have shallow roots and be unable to stand when a strong wind of adversity comes.

Since your job is to prepare your team for hurricanes of adversity, each person needs to build his or her own skills. Each needs to grow independently skillful before they can function as a mature team player.

Peer pressure is a strong motivator for your strong-willed child to obey the rules. Usually a quick comment from a team member will be enough to remind your rebellious child that he is loosing team rewards. If he continues to choose to misbehave, he may have decided that this negative power is what he wants. In that case, he may have to be taken off the team system so he can be individually rewarded or punished with points.

In brief: Your rewards and your punishments are usually measured in time. Rebellion gets double punishment: time in same day grounding (and/or spanking) and time off awards activities (which may also be on the same day, for a small or immature child).

Team points can motivate a rebel to see his impact on brothers or sisters. He will be more apt to comply unless he is using his negative power against the team. In that case, his rebellion will not disappear. You will want to separate his negative points, divorcing him from the team. Perhaps a better idea is to reward the team with a point when the rebel is able to behave well—for perhaps 15 or 30 minutes.

Think Through and Practice Your Back-up Strategy

You will want to think through your series of back-up actions if the above scenario doesn't bring results over a period of a month.

There are many consequences for rebellion. If rebellion is a primary, longstanding issue, you might have to get initial compliance by isolating the child from any audience (siblings or friends) and/or by removing stimuli like TV and game time.

Grounding is often an emotional time, so you will want to prepare your child for that possibility if teamwork is not part of her "game plan for life."

I noticed difficulty once my sons re-entered public school in the fall. My summer discipline was weakened by peer pressure. After one semester's probation and warning, I homeschooled my sons in order to control peer influence. I placed responsibility for their education squarely on them. When they were held accountable for two school years they learned that their education was not a joke or something they could slide through.

One son completed his high school education by age 17 while working full-time at McDonald's to earn spending money. With that money he bought a car, computer, television and a lot of self respect. His SAT scores were high enough in middle school to encourage the University at Denver to offer him college level coursework. He chose flight training in the Navy and the adventure that offered instead of college. Then he earned college credit in the Navy. His two combat medals were not part of my plan!

Homeschooling gave both sons the self-confidence to know they could choose any career path and be successful. They can "think outside the box" because they had enrichment on top of the required coursework. They would not have had that enriched learning sitting in a classroom when they were so restless.

Now in their early 30's, they both make a good income at work they love. The lessons are two fold: First, natural consequences are a great way to teach when they are controlled by the parent. Secondly, parents must commit their dreams for their children to God.

> Removing privileges is not abusive when it is done in love, without the kind of verbal put-downs which frustrated pushover parents often use. Their passive, poorly thought through discipline ends up with verbal abuse. Your stress-free discipline avoids that.

The key here is to frustrate the child rather than the parent, but without anger and smoldering resentments. You want to minimize emotional pain that may evolve later into underhanded, unmanageable destructive behavior. Make expectations clear, walk through them in detail, set deadlines. Then give consequences. See also if you can spot the triggers for disobedience. It is possible your child is over-stimulated or overwhelmed.

Other possibilities for backing up your strategy include spanking. Spanking is biblical. The following notes supporting spanking were taken from a discussion by Drs. Meier and Laramore in an October 29, 2002 radio broadcast by Focus on the Family, KPRZ, San Diego radio 1210 AM: Once boundaries are outlined, judicious administration of spanking (1 to 2 swats for a two to six-year-old) for deliberate defiance (not for accidents or typical childish behavior) is all right. If children defy the rules in public, defer consequences until you are in private. Explain the rule; apply the consequence—in the absence of anger. Show grace after the punishment.

Effectiveness of spanking: Spanking must be judiciously applied by people who have no anger management or impulse control problems and no history of abuse. According to Dr. James Dobson, judicious spanking actually results in less violence in the upbringing of a child than the various types of abuse—including verbal—which are statistically applied by those who never spank.

Dobson continues by saying that spanking should disappear after age six, when other consequences should be more effective. When the spanking is finished, hug your child, assuring him or her that you love them. Explain that their behavior is not acceptable.

- Develop strength of character in your child to eliminate the need for spanking. As parents, you will move from dictatorship to democracy as the child matures. Husband and wife need to be on the same page about discipline. Discuss rules together ahead of time. Crisis discipline is unreasonable.

Make eye contact, get in their personal space, and use the body language sequence already explained.

Positive alternatives to spanking include *effective* use of time-out (as boring as possible, enforce isolation without attention). Don't get mad; get boring. Be prepared to hang in there with your child: "Time-out only starts when you stop whining and complaining." Be consistent in order to be effective.

It is important to be alert, aware, and educated about your child's ability. I recommend the monthly packet of games and sequential parenting tips and newsletter "Focus on Your Child." Learn about this at www.focusonyourchild.com or write Focus on the Family, Colorado Springs, CO 80995. Phone: (800) 232-6459. This is an ideal detailed series of journals and audio.

Visit Family.org to search for spanking links and articles. Consider buying 🕮 *The New Dare to Discipline*, by Dr. James Dobson. Ask for a free booklet called "Questions Parents have About Discipline." It covers subjects like how to set limits, corporal punishment, and developmentally appropriate discipline.

Rebellion and negotiation are complex ideas. How do we help a child discern between rebellion and simple forgetfulness? When a child does not do something we ask, there are only two possibilities: he can't, or he won't.

If he has been carefully taught and deliberately chooses not to obey, that is rebellion. He must pay a price too high for comfort. We have to read his body language when he is confused and when he is rebellious.

➥ We must observe our child to find out exactly how long his attention span is when he is paying attention to something he likes, such as a game or TV program. We must notice his body language, facial expression, eye contact when he is trying to evade us and when he is being cooperative. Then we must point out to him what those markers of rebellion are when we see them.

It is a good idea when we see examples of rebellion in the Bible to share these stories with our children. Cain is an example of someone who could have told God he was sorry for the offering which was not according to God's specifications. Instead, Cain got angry at God and jealous of his brother. It is normal to feel angry when we are frustrated, you can explain. But the Bible says, "Be angry but do not sin" (Ephesians 4:26). Explain to your child that God loves us and gives us the strength to resist rebellion when we are angry.

While it is important for us to recognize, listen to, and respect a child's ideas, we are still obligated to govern our children until they mature in judgment and ability. There can be no tolerance for rebellion—deliberate disobedience. Do not cave in on this one. Rebellion can be identified by repeated, open defiance. It only gets worse with practice. Do not allow your child to force or charm or negotiate you into one single exception to the rules.

Judge by the fruit: Negotiating can be used for good or bad purposes: to reinforce family goals or fragment family unity.

If a child's negotiation is successfully used for selfish ends, the family is fractured while the child loses faith in family boundaries. If a child holds his cooperation out to the parent as a reward for parental "goodies," the whole fabric of family respect and cooperation is shredded. "I'll be good in public if you'll let me watch Dynamic Duo tonight," is not acceptable. That's coercion, and needs to be punished for what it is: rebellion.

The right counselor can help. If family counseling seems called for, do not hesitate to get it, but seek out a Christian counselor. Discuss the severity of your issues and interview the counselor before setting an appointment.

A thorough family counselor does not merely present a sounding board for severe complaints and then tell you what he or she recommends. The best counselors will use various methods to analyze each family member's personality, communication style, anger management style, self-image, and concept development. This initial evaluation should not take more than 1-1/2 hours, and should result in an individualized therapy plan for each member of the family. We can all become more effective, proactive and loving in our personal interactions. Depending on our own family background, this will take more or less practice.

Supportive Solutions

Supportive solutions are an essential part of your back-up discipline. Explore different solutions if your children are adamant and opposed to change on an issue you know is important.

> Remember that when change occurs in families your children will not be the only ones opposed to it! Often parents or grandparents have problems with positive changes that they know need to occur. It takes 32 days to change a bad habit into a good one. That is why parental accountability—the Parents' Chart—is so important.

Supportive solutions, then, go beyond this system into the specific, creative answers needed by your family. They involve "I win-You win" ideas. When you are in the A-Zone you are not likely to come up with supportive solutions. That is another reason you need to practice the deep breathing as often as you feel any stress during your day.

If discussion is hot and nobody can suggest a supportive solution, agree to separate, pray and reconvene in a family meeting. Then brainstorm, with everyone giving possible solutions.

Write down all solutions, without positive or negative comment on the merits of the ideas. Look for examples like your dilemma in the Bible. Look for biblical principles to apply or commands to follow. Then discuss the pros and cons of your ideas in detail. Is the idea true or false factually? Is it practical or impractical, affordable, expensive in time or money? Use the criteria for solving problems that I have included in the Appendix. Work through the problem-solving matrix one bit at a time.

Non-negotiable Items

Remember that you are the authority, the last word, despite the wrong ideas that your child receives from misguided teachers and sitcoms. If your child believes he is equal to you, remind him that he's not mature enough to have mastered Youth Expectations 5, (much less the parent's level). He is not financially independent, cannot sign a business contract, vote or buy a home. You are preparing him for the time when those choices will be his to make. Then his opinion will carry equal weight with yours. Now it is your job to prepare him for that time. His job is to perfect his skills so he doesn't get frustrated as an adult by spending too much time doing normal chores. Ignorance is never bliss, unless you are a dependent child.

Trying to reason with a rebellious teen feels like negotiating with a terrorist. There is no middle ground for a rebellious teen. Remember, you must stay out of the A-Zone. The adrenalin rush that is part of an angry debate is not good for any of you. You will loose access to all your skills when you are functioning out of your primitive brain stem. Nobody wins such an argument. You do not even make sense to yourself.

When you lose your temper, revert to the pattern you have practiced with your learning partner: slow movements, deep breathing, silence, etc. If you have said or done things which are unchristian, apologize to your children and ask their forgiveness. Put yourself into computer mode. Put off policy decisions until everyone is rested and focused.

Parents, do not explain, defend or negotiate once you have taken a reasoned stand. You choose the issues and the battleground. Choose your battles carefully.

Moral issues are clearly more important than whether your child pierces her ears, colors her hair green, or wears black nail polish. Low cut tops and high cut skirts can be quietly modified if both mom and daughter shop together and both must approve the wardrobe. It must be something your child wants and Mom can live with.

Look ahead a few years to anticipate what the issues will be, and decide on your "game plan" before they come up. Then express your concern to your children before they are personally involved in the issues. Be realistic about peer pressure and the big sell of commercial interests, explaining these stresses before they become personal stresses.

> If you need counseling help, get it. The only shame is in staying stuck in a bad place.

Avoid posturing and nagging. As Cynthia Tobias says, we give too many warnings and not enough tickets as parents. You can guess the result when the police do this: obedience becomes a joke. Order does not exist. The same thing happens in your family.

Remember: You know best what's good for your child, with the help of scriptural precepts that have worked for centuries. You have the experience to see what's around the corner, because you've traveled that road before. Perhaps you have learned from someone else's sad experience. True stories—without names attached—will give credence to what you require of your child.

Acting Out: What If It Does Not Stop?

If your child is "acting out" both at school and at home, it is important to rule out the possibility that your child may have a biochemical imbalance. Investigate the book by Dr. Michael R. Lyon, M.D. and Dr. G. Christine Laurell, Ph.D., 📖 *Is Your Child's Brain Starving?* It is available in health food stores and in Barnes and Noble. Food sensitivities, colon irregularities (even without a stomachache), parasites (you worm your pet monthly, don't you? Critters travel and are hard to diagnose) and other problems may be holding your child back in school and in responses to your discipline.[60] Biological stressors place great pressure on the brain.

If your child is "acting out" only at school or church, you may have created a home environment that is not open to solving his problems. If it is difficult for your child to express feelings openly at home, those feelings will go "underground" and will surface in problem behavior outside the home.

However, the problem behavior at school may not be the result of unresolved family issues. Bullying and other school-related problems may be causing tardiness, clowning in class, and other discipline challenges.

You may want to request a "staffing." It involves a meeting of you and your child with teachers, school counselor, and possibly a doctor—at no charge to you. Sometimes a few simple changes will create an open communication environment at home, and better accommodation by teachers. Other recommended activities may free your child to behave better at school.

However, bear in mind that subconscious conflict between the materialistic humanism taught at school and your biblical concepts lived at home may be the cause of conflict at home and at school.

In such a case, your child will behave better and be happier if you homeschool him or her. Homeschooling is legal in most states, and your State Board of Education has guidelines with approved textbooks. You will find that there is a large supportive group of parents doing homeschooling, and they often coordinate on labs, field trips and sporting activities. Their children score high on the SAT and PSAT tests required for college entrance. They perform better on standardized tests at every age level than public school students do.

> Homeschooled students have time for part-time jobs, museums, and many other field trips, because there is no wasted time. A full day's work is easily done in half a day, and the rest of the day is open for enrichment.

If your child is "acting out" at school, and you have considered all of the above, ask yourself about your parenting style. Unreasonably authoritarian parents who do not establish a love relationship with their children will find themselves in parent-teacher conferences and other undesirable situations—such as meetings with a probation officer. Remember, rules without relationship cause rebellion.

The best place for your child to "act out" his frustrations, anger, and fear is at home. Sometimes your active listening, quality time, and prayer are the only things needed to solve problems.

In short: There are no short cuts to successful discipline. As you reread this section, highlight your weak areas and discuss them with your learning partner, spouse, pastor or counselor—or all of the above people. Pick one weak spot per month to monitor, and ask for feedback from people close to you. Write every small step in the right direction in your victory journal.

Enjoy the Price of Sainthood: Impulse Control and Attention Span

Attention span must be increased—yours and that of your child! Have you shortened your attention span and ability to focus by watching television for hours every day? Do you prefer a life without the hard work of thinking through details? Educational game time will help both of you increase your focus and attention span.

Impulse control must be practiced. We are the models. Are we adults always looking for an easy life without any effort—pleasures without our sacrifice of time and energy? That is not realistic. There is no free lunch. There is always a price to be paid. Mature adults learn to enjoy the price. The process of earning our pleasures becomes our journey to sainthood.

That is why family teamwork is so important. In a very real way, it is a model of real world frustrations, effort and victories. Failures and tears are part of the process. Godliness is not awarded us for doing nothing.

> Happiness depends upon adjusting our goals and our desires to fit reality, and having the courage to submit all to the control of Christ. Where is fast fun and lazy thinking—entertainment and immediate gratification—in that picture? Let us be slaves to Christ rather than to our own sin.[61]

Impulse control needs to be carefully taught, like negotiation skills and obedience. Let your child know you are still practicing these skills, and learning more about how to use them well. Begin all teaching with teens from a point of your own weakness.[62] Yes! While God has given you authority over your child, you want your children to know that you are teachable. When you make a mistake you will admit it and correct it.

Humility on your part will help your child understand (and you need to say this) that we are all God's children, responsible to Him for what we do.

We all need help from the Holy Spirit and from each other to do life God's way. Remind your child that you need his help, and then tell him how he can help you.

If teaching impulse control, for example, tell him that you've gained eight pounds (or want to eat more healthy food) and need his help in reminding you not to eat cookies.[63] Impulse control is a lifelong challenge. Moses was still struggling with his temper when he was in his 80's. That is why he could not enter the Promised Land.

Your exchange of insight and accountability with your child will motivate you to achieve better than a stack of self-help books. At the same time, you are doing sneaky skill building with your child.

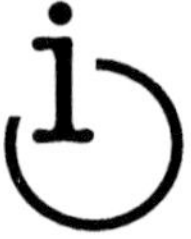

In short: Make your simplified expectations available to your child when you ask his help. Your child will be happy to help you get rid of a few bad habits by marking on a Point Chart similar to the one you use for him. Your reward for positive performance is educational game time with your child![64]

Win the Reward: Lasting Love

The bottom line: Rules without relationship equal rebellion. If you don't spend time with your children outside of discipline mode, you will not have a good relationship. They will know that you don't care about who they really are. They will rightly conclude that you don't love them. They will not accept your beliefs or your discipline.

When they get a chance they will undermine both with passive aggression—sneaky disobedience. To prevent this, have fun playing without any objective in mind, doing what each child enjoys, not what you want him or her to enjoy. Then your child will want to please you.

> ➥ Remember, your love relationship with your child does not mean breaking the rules. Love is not permissiveness.

God's love is unconditional, but He always makes us live with the results of our poor choices. Your love can be unconditional, but must have consequences for poor choices. If a child expects to escape discipline by saying he or she is sorry, remind him of this fact. The points go in a negative column just as they do when we're sorry we ran that red light. We still must pay the fine. Your child must still take negative points.

Use These Tips

Do this program with a friend. Get together with your learning partner, spouse, neighbor or someone close to you. That way, you can share success stories and ideas that work for each of you, and—most importantly—keep each other going when the temptation arises to quit. It is also important that other caregivers for your child do the same program. Get on the same page!

Remember to check quality control: You will give your child points based on how complete his job was—on a scale of one to two—with two being the best possible job. Evaluate an incomplete job by saying, "That was a 'one'. Next time you might practice for a 'two.'"

Keep the old charts. This is a record of how much your child has helped you over time. Review and praise progress often. Whenever you feel like no progress has been made, get out those old charts and review them. Remember with delight, for example, that six months ago your child had you trained to wake her up and make her bed, but now she's doing it herself!

You may have to work for a week or two on getting your child to obey the first time he is told a command. It's worth the battle. Just be patient and persistent. Every skill learned now will be a joy later. Every bad habit will be a curse magnified later.

Write down your areas of challenge here.

____

____

Prioritize them using the priority matrix in the Appendix.

Tackle one area per month.

Reward yourself with time off for good behavior. Get a sitter and spend time away from the frenzy of chores and duties. A half-day per week of dining out, a concert, a hobby, the library, etc., will do wonders.

Section III

What Must We Do To Put Stress-free Discipline into Practice?

Establish Goals

Your goals must be measurable, realistic, and have positive consequences. They should be written. Goals must be clearly defined, with an example to show what the definition means.

Dwell on definitions: Post them and be precise. After introducing and discussing every definition, find applications and examples. Let silence fall after you have told a story or given an example. Ask for two more examples.

Then ask, "What would result if__________?" Exercise the question. What would happen if someone did not use impulse control? What are some examples of impulse control problems? What does God think about impulse control? Are people judged for not having impulse control? (Consider Moses after he hit the rock at Mariba in anger.)

Impulse control: You might define impulse control using this model. Impulse control is a type of good behavior with the following characteristics:

- A person waits, rather than reacting to a situation or challenge,
- Thinking through the effects of different actions
- And choosing the action with the best long-term consequences for everyone involved.

For example, there is good impulse control when a teenager chooses to go with the family to clean and paint an elderly person's home rather than to sit watching cartoons. Why? Discuss impulse control with your learning partner.

Follow This System for Introducing the Charts

Assumptions: You have already obtained the appropriate Expectations and Point Charts, and have thought and walked through your routine according to the above basics. It is a relief to know that all you have to do to be an outstanding parent is stay one step ahead of your child.

Step One

Use no parents' charts at first, only Children's Point Chart 1 and Children's Expectations 1. When the chores are too hard for your child, take some of the harder ones for yourself, and add them onto your child's duties next month when you are both familiar with the routine. We do not want underhanded anger and passive aggression created by unrealistic expectations.

Begin with Point Chart 1 and Expectations 1 even if you have teenagers.[65] Impulse control is a key problem at any age, and so is the challenge of making messes, leaving things out, breakfast and bedtime, etc. You will walk through each chore in detail, one skill at a time. Practice that for a few days, and then teach a second skill. Do Expectations 1 until you and your children (or teens) have all concepts mastered, perhaps two weeks or longer. Right now your main interest is to create a habit of accountability for them, and to reinforce your habit of being consistent about your basic rules. (Grace is given up-front before the day starts. Then, pushover parents, it's time for law.) Do Expectations 1 if there is anything on the list which needs practice.

If you wish to create your own Expectations Lists, please do not do this until the third month you have this system in place. Then you may list the additional chores on a separate chart or at the bottom of the set I have given you. Good manners are scored under impulse control.

Step Two

After one month of practice with this system, introduce Parents' Point Chart 1 and stay on Children's Point Chart 1, adding whatever chores you held back the first month. Note the charts which follow this section. Parents' Point Chart 1 only concerns impulse control: doing one essential chore. Choose from those related to food, health or safety.

Define exactly what single part of your long Expectations List is giving you trouble, and ask your child to help remind you to do that one task. If you are beginning with a three-year-old, you might say you need help remembering to put on your safety belt or some other simple task related to food, safety, or health. For an older child, you might say that you wish help in remembering to plan healthy meals, and need 5-8 servings of fruit and vegetables on the table every day. Daddy needs 9 servings.

Help your child measure out a serving. A serving is one cup raw, a medium-sized piece of fruit or one half cup cooked fruit or vegetable. These things are measurable and have positive consequences. Your child should realistically be able to count to eight, know what foods are fruits and vegetables, and know what a cup measure looks like. That way, nobody is expected to do more than he is able. Yet each child knows how important he is to the family as a whole.

Keep it short, painless for the child to remember, and simple. Make it literal and touchable. Intangibles come later. Teaching tips related to various age groups are in the Appendix. They will help you know what is "normal" for each age group.

Step Three

Step three occurs whenever the child has mastered Point Chart 1. At the "graduation ceremony" you will introduce Parents' Point Chart 2, your second Parents' Expectations List (you may design this one) and Children's Point Chart 2 with Children's Expectations 2. Point Chart 2 has space for extra points if a job is done fast and well. This is up to you, but if a child races against time, have him race himself, not his brother or sister's time. You'll need to remind the child there are no points if they say they did the chore but it's been messed up before they called you to check on it.

Here they are:

Children's Expectations List 2

- Put pajamas away and take laundry to basket. Help by sorting family laundry into whites, darks, sheets/towels and print piles on laundry day. Hang up clothing which is not dirty. Hang jackets on hooks. Put games, toys and books onto toy shelf.
- Make your own bed (facilitated by $15 sheet fasteners on corners).
- Empty your own trash basket and one other.
- Take your own dishes and one other to the table and off again later. (Five or six-year-old children can set the table and clear it later, especially with a picture in front of them to show them where the dishes and flatware, salt and pepper, etc., go. Put the picture on cardboard, hung on a nail on the inside of a lower cabinet.)
- Brush teeth after meals.
- Wash face and ears with soap and water. Hang up towels and face cloths neatly.
- Dry up water spilled on bathroom floor with mop or big under-sink sponge.
- Help an adult wash dishes by scraping food into trash, loading dishwasher, washing or drying.
- Stack or shelve magazines or books neatly in the living rooms as well in the child's rooms after helping with dinner. Ask to be excused when finished.

Children's Point Chart 2

– Negative Points		+ Positive Points	
Making a Mess (Spilling without wiping up, unmade bed, or leaving clothing, toys, etc., around while starting something else)	- 1 each	**Cleaning Up** (Taking out trash, brushing teeth, carrying plates to sink, putting things away, helping others work.)	+2 each
Impulse Control Problem (Example: hitting, grabbing, insults, backtalk)	-2 each	**Impulse Control and/or Teamwork** (Following directions or "I felt like ___, but instead I did this ___ for our benefit")	+3 each
Poor Breakfast or Late Breakfast, or Late Bedtime	- 1 each	**Healthy Breakfast** On Time and/or In Bed On Time.	+2 each
Any Lie	- 1 each	**Truth Telling** (when it hurts and is to your disadvantage)	+2 each
Note: Outright Rebellion gets double consequences 1) Immediate down time or spanking and 2) Points off on the chart	-2 each specific instance	Always start out with positive points – these are Grace Points	Grace Points +10
Negative Points Total	______	Positive Points Total minus Negative Points Total Total Reward Points	________ – ________ +/- _____

Expectations 2 for Parents

These will be items you are asking your child to help you with. Pick one item the first month, two when children graduate to their next chart, etc.

- Make breakfast, box lunches, dinner.
- Include 5-8 servings of fruit and vegetables for the day.
- Carry out morning devotional. (Give your child his own alarm clock for this.)

Parents' Point Chart 2

– Negative Points		+ Positive Points	
Ignoring Chores or Making a Mess (Including breakfast and sleep schedule, spilling without wiping up, unmade bed, litter, unfinished work, etc.)	- 1 each	**Cleaning Up or Doing Chores Without Being Told** (Now includes breakfast and sleep on schedule, taking out trash, brushing teeth, carrying plates to sink, putting things away, helping others work.)	+2 each
Impulse Control Problem (Example: hitting, grabbing, insults, backtalk, unnecessary anger)	-2 each	**Impulse Control and/or Teamwork** ("I felt like ___, but instead I did this ____ for our benefit", healthy anger manage-ment/problem solving)	+3 each
Any Lie	- 1 each	**Truth Telling** (When it hurts and is to your disadvantage)	+2 each
Coercion (I win, you lose; using force or threats)	- 1 each	**Win-win Negotiation** (Let's plan to do ___, taking turns, etc.)	+2 each
Note: Outright Rebellion gets double consequences 1) Immediate down time or spanking and 2) Points off on the chart	-2 each specific instance	Always start out with positive points – these are Grace Points	Grace Points +10
Negative Points Total	_____	Positive Points Total	________
		minus	–
		Negative Points Total	________
		Total Reward Points	+/- _____

Parents' Point Chart 2 is a bit more of a challenge. After all, if you can expect it of your child, you must model it also. On impulse control, share one or two examples of the specific parenting skills that challenge you, but keep it brief and tangible like that above. Find one or two occasions when you tend to "lose it," when you need reminders to stay on target. Concrete thinking is the only thinking young people find comfortable, so be very specific.

You define your bad habits. You might ask help from an older child on one or two impulse control problems; perhaps those related to savings, tithing, careful stewardship of money, etc.

> ➥ You make the list, focusing on one habit at a time until the skill is mastered—until it's automatic. Then move on to the next challenge.

Possibly there are times when you get uncontrollably angry; throw things, scream, and use bad language, unnecessary force or threats. You may have times when you ignore essential chores. As you aim for self-improvement, you need to list what those essential chores are, and what uncontrolled anger looks like. Post definitions where everyone can see them. Review them daily.

Make every effort to exercise good impulse control most of the time, since you are the model. If you can't get to bed at a reasonable hour and eat a good breakfast, it is not fair to expect your child to do it! Interdependence means teamwork with the Lord's objectives in mind: self-control is a major goal.[66]

Ignoring essential chores is a type of irresponsible behavior with the following characteristics:

- The chores are vitally important to family food, health or safety.
- Not doing them causes family members or pets to be cheated out of a healthy lifestyle.
- Not doing them results in threat or danger to a family member or pet.
- Things only get worse when the chores are not done.
- Ignoring these chores causes emotional stress in children—children may decide that they do not want to grow up.

Uncontrolled anger is a type of unhealthy behavior with the following characteristics:

- The angry person screams, throw things, uses bad language, unnecessary force or threats.
- Adrenaline causes stress on the body, blood pressure goes up, breathing and heart rates increase, whites of the eyes show, and neck and shoulders tense up, while the angry person wants to fight or run away from the problem.
- The angry person shows this behavior for longer than three minutes.
- He/she does not try to find any solution to the problem that is good for everyone.
- Unresolved problems lead to angry outbursts and depression.
- Anger is a physical response to pain, frustration or fear.

Step Four

The next Parents' Point Chart 3 includes doing essential chores, messes, impulse control, and truth telling or loving confrontation. This correlates with the Children's Chart 3. The Children's Chart 3 includes issues related to lying...but not limited to lying. Your child is now held responsible for any lie or deliberate oversight.

Begin practicing and identifying healthy assertiveness for and with your child. Your child must learn to lovingly tell the truth, regardless of consequences. This is healthy assertiveness, not sociopathic aggression. We want to reward the practice of diplomatic, loving confrontation. Many adults have never learned this. That is why it is on your chart!

At this point you are defining lying for your child, but if your child is young or immature, he may not be able to apply this idea to his "stories." Also, you will want to train him to resist telling Grandma that she has whiskers and is unkissable.

It is now time for you to create your own definition:

What are white lies?

- They avoid unnecessary, unloving statements which hurt feelings.
- They express social graces, good manners, tact.
- They usually deal with small issues, with no bad effects on others.
- They may be used in serious situations to save lives.

You will work on concepts related to lying a little at a time, without being too harsh on a pre-school child but using each incident as a learning experience. Have your child identify diplomacy and non-diplomatic situations. You will want to show the difference between a deliberate untruth and an unavoidable situation.

For example, you promised to pick up your child after the party but did not come when you said you would. Your car broke down. That situation was beyond your control. Have your child learn to recognize lies enough to apply terms to you, then help him transfer that learning to his own behavior as he matures. You will want to monitor and confirm all of his school situations, since lying which goes undetected will become a bad habit. Your lack of awareness may in that case reinforce weak character.

Lying is a type of communication (spoken or unspoken) with the following characteristics:

- It deliberately misleads another person with untruth by what is said or what is left unsaid with negative consequences, such as causing pain to the other person (not merely offense, which I consider a choice on the other person's part).
- It results in a future lack of trust in the relationship,
- It results in dysfunctional anger, fear or frustration.
- It causes love to die one lie at a time.
- It is an effort to avoid responsibility for poor choices.
- It fails to trust God for consequences of telling the truth.

Coercion is a type of aggression with the following characteristics:

- Force or threat of violence is used against another person.
- It may include nonverbal communication or physical threat.
- It dominates another by nullifying their will.

Aggression is a type of hostile behavior against another person with the following characteristics:

- It may include physical opposition, nonverbal and verbal domination or humiliation to get what the aggressor wants.
- It may include a sneer or look of scorn, a disgusted snort or sigh to show disdain of another person in order to get superiority over that person.
- Verbal aggression includes blaming, insults, put-downs, profanity and sarcasm (see James 3:5-10).
- Passive aggression includes moving against another person or manipulating others to get one's own way or to get even, and to express what the aggressor is unwilling to say outright.
- Passive aggression includes procrastinating, forgetting, dawdling, pouting, manipulative tears and the silent treatment IF THESE ARE DELIBERATELY USED TO GET ONE'S OWN WAY.[67]

None of us is free of passive aggression, but children need to understand by careful teaching what tactics they are using to get their way. We cannot let them succeed in getting their own way by aggressive tactics.

We parents need to restrain our own aggression, the immature tactics we use when we feel frustrated. We all need to get our brains into computer mode, stay out of the A-Zone, and solve our problems rather than allow them to recycle over and over for years. We do not want to rehearse sin. Home fellowships are the ideal place to build true problem-solving habits.

The Christian lifestyle is a constructive way of living and relating to others. Assertive behavior honors us and others. We are caring for others and pleasing God by caring for ourselves as well. We seek to be honest, real, direct, open and loving. The true Christian will work toward seeing himself as important in God's eyes, with valid feelings, ideas, and rights to expressing those.[68] Humility is not humiliation. God did not design us to be doormats. We need to train ourselves with help from God to accept others without putting ourselves down.

Take a look at those charts which follow. Visualize your family all helping each other to grow in these areas.

Children's Expectations List 3 (Ages 7-10 and older)[69]

- Put pajamas away and take laundry to basket. Hang up clothing which is not dirty. Hang jackets on hooks. Put toys, books, etc. onto toy shelf. Make bed (facilitated by $15 sheet fasteners on corners).
- Help by washing, drying, folding and putting away one load of family laundry after sorting into whites, darks, sheets/towels and pale print piles on laundry day. Place parents' folded clothing in parents' room, kitchen linens in appropriate kitchen drawer, etc.
- Empty your own trash basket and one other.
- Set the table and clear it later. Help make breakfast. Make salads for dinner.
- Brush your teeth after meals. Wash bathroom basin daily, drying chrome to a shine.
- Sweep in kitchen and dining room (if bare floors) after dinner. Empty kitchen trash outside.
- Help an adult wash dishes by scraping food into trash, loading dishwasher, washing or drying.
- Stack or shelve magazines or books neatly in the living rooms as well in children's rooms, after helping with dinner. Put anything of yours into a bag to go to your room. Report back to parent and ask to be excused when finished.[70]

- Do homework. Show it and your notebook or backpack to your parents. If it's not all neat and complete, do homework over.[71] Organize stuff into files: English, Math, Science, etc. Put big assignments on family calendar.
- Shower or bathe on family schedule. Hang up towels and face cloths neatly. Dry up water spilled on bathroom or kitchen floors with mop or big under-sink sponge.
- Feed the family pet.
- Clean pet's areas once a week.
- Vacuum as directed.

Children's Point Chart 3 (ages 7-10)

– Negative Points		+ Positive Points	
Ignoring Chores or Making a Mess (Including breakfast and sleep schedule, spilling without wiping up, unmade bed, litter, unfinished work, etc.)	- 1 each	**Cleaning Up or Doing Chores Without Being Told** (Now includes breakfast and sleep on schedule, taking out trash, brushing teeth, carrying plates to sink, putting things away, helping others work.)	+2 each
Impulse Control Problem (Example: hitting, grabbing, insults, backtalk, unnecessary anger)	-2 each	**Impulse Control and/or Teamwork** ("I felt like ___, but instead I did this ____ for our benefit", healthy anger manage-ment/problem solving)	+3 each
Any Lie	- 1 each	**Truth Telling** (When it hurts and is to your disadvantage)	+2 each
Coercion (I win, you lose; using force or threats)	- 1 each	**Win-win Negotiation** (Let's plan to do ___, taking turns, etc.)	+2 each
Note: Outright Rebellion gets double consequences 1) Immediate down time or spanking and 2) Points off on the chart	-2 each specific instance	Always start out with positive points – these are Grace Points	Grace Points +10
Negative Points Total	______	Positive Points Total minus Negative Points Total Total Reward Points	________ - ________ +/- _____

Youth Expectations List 4 (for ages 11-13 and older)[72]

- Put pajamas away and take laundry to basket. Hang up clothing which is not dirty. Hang jackets on hooks. Put toys, books, etc. onto toy shelf. Make bed (facilitated by $15 sheet fasteners on corners).
- Help by washing, drying, folding and putting away one load of family laundry after sorting into whites, darks, sheets/towels and pale print piles on laundry day. Place parents' folded clothing in parents' room, kitchen linens in appropriate kitchen drawer, etc.
- Empty your own trash basket and one other.
- Set the table and clear it later. Help make breakfast. Make salads for dinner.
- Brush your teeth after meals. Wash bathroom basin daily, drying chrome to a shine.
- Sweep in kitchen and dining room (if bare floors) after dinner. Empty kitchen trash outside.
- Help an adult wash dishes by scraping food into trash, loading dishwasher, washing or drying.
- Stack or shelve magazines or books neatly in the living rooms as well in children's rooms, after helping with dinner. Put anything of yours into a bag to go to your room. Report back to parent and ask to be excused when finished.
- Do homework. Show it and your notebook or backpack to your parents.[73] If it's not all neat and complete, do homework over.[74]
- Shower or bathe on family schedule. Hang up towels and face cloths neatly. Dry up water spilled on bathroom or kitchen floors with mop or big under-sink sponge.
- Feed the family pet.
- Clean pet's areas once a week.
- Vacuum as directed.

Ignoring unpleasant truths, or failing to confront wrong behavior is behavior that your child can "ping" you for. On the other hand, loving confrontation earns you positive points. Once you learn loving confrontation, your marriage and your evangelism will benefit.

You lose nothing but your bad habits. You have made a Parents' Expectations list to suit yourself. Your point chart looks like this:

Youth Point Chart 4 (ages 11-13)

– Negative Points		+ Positive Points	
Ignoring Chores or Making a Mess (Including breakfast and sleep schedule, spilling without wiping up, unmade bed, litter, unfinished work.)	- 1 each	**Cleaning Up or Doing Chores Without Being Told** (Includes breakfast and sleep on schedule, washing dishes, putting things away, helping others work)	+2 each
Impulse Control Problem (ignoring essential chores, unnecessary anger)	-2 each	**Impulse Control and/or Teamwork** ("I felt like ___, but instead I did this ____ for our benefit", healthy anger management/problem solving)	+3 each
Softie Love (Not confronting moral situations with unpleasant truth, or lying to escape a moral dilemma)	- 1 each	**Truth in love** (Telling the truth when it hurts – particularly when it is to your disadvantage)	+2 each
Coercion (I win, you lose; using force or threats)	- 1 each	**Win-win Negotiation** (Let's plan to do ___, taking turns, etc.)	+2 each

continued next page

– Negative Points		+ Positive Points	
Note: Outright Rebellion gets double consequences 1) Immediate down time or spanking and 2) Points off on the chart	-2 each specific instance	**Swift Obedience** (obedience within 3 seconds)	+ 2 points
Time-out (lost time for disobedience, Ping Time)	(1 point per lost minute)	**Bonus Points** (given for maintaining a positive total yesterday)	+2 each
		Always start out with positive points – these are Grace Points	Grace Points +10
Negative Points Total	______	Positive Points Total minus Negative Points Total Total Reward Points	______ – ______ +/- ______

Loving confrontation is a type of tough love with the following characteristics:

- It is clear, concise, and done without an audience of friends or family,
- It details the type of poor choice or behavior problem which needs correction,
- Problem behavior has been explained and right behavior has been rehearsed ahead of time,
- It proposes a way to train the person who needs to make correction,
- It is done in a loving manner.

Step Five

The Parents' Point Chart 4 includes win-win negotiation (supportive solutions,) as well as all of the above issues. These may need months and years of practice. Be patient with yourself. God is not finished yet.

Supportive solutions are a type of problem-solving behavior with the following characteristics:

- They present win-win answers to a dilemma (everyone wins) with added emotional support.
- They consider the needs, personalities and desires of those involved.
- They prevent crises, solving problems before they arise (proactive).
- They are built on perceiving and honoring each person's basic issues or needs and concerns whether these are "logical" or not.
- They result in stronger trust, love and family unity.
- Solutions may include negotiation skills useful outside the family.

For example, suppose someone leaves the gate open and the family dog disappears. Supportive solutions may result from a blame-free environment where the family brainstorms ideas on how each person can help solve the problem. Computer whiz Carrie volunteers to make up and post wanted posters with Fido's face on them. Mom phones Animal Control and the neighbors to see if she can locate the dog. Ten-year-old Sam rides through the neighborhood on his bike, etc.

A win-win solution is a type of negotiation that has the following characteristics:

- It provides an answer where everyone wins, nobody loses.
- It has no criticism or negative judgment which makes people angry and defensive.

- It is practical, addressing the real issues which are causing conflict.
- It is fair to everyone, so conflict is resolved.
- It does not have to be emotionally satisfying, but must be fair.[75]

Step Six

This is the final set of charts. By now your children have achieved college-level thinking skills and are gaining adult skills to a degree which will amaze you. Here are the Expectations and Point Charts.

Youth Expectations List 5 for Ages 14-18 and Up[76]

- Put pajamas away and take laundry to basket. Make bed. Hang up clothing which is not dirty. Put misplaced items away before school and before bed.
- Wash, dry, fold and put away two loads of family laundry after sorting into whites, darks, sheets/towels and print piles on laundry day. Place parents' folded clothing in parents' room, kitchen linens in appropriate kitchen drawer, etc.
- Empty own trash basket and one other.
- Set the table and clear it later. Help make breakfast. Make salads, etc., for dinner.
- Sweep in kitchen and dining room (if bare floors) after dinner.
- Empty kitchen trash outside.
- Wash dishes as directed.
- Stack or shelve magazines or books neatly in the living rooms as well as in own room after helping with dinner. Put anything of yours which is out of place into a bag to go to your room. Report back to parent and ask to be excused when finished. Do homework.

- Show homework to parents and your notebook or backpack to your parents. If work is not all neat and complete, do homework over.[77] Organize returned papers into home files: English, Math, Science, etc. Organize notebooks in order, old papers behind newest ones. Put big assignments on family calendar.
- Wash bathroom basin daily, drying chrome to a shine.
- Feed the family pet.
- Clean pet's areas once a week.
- Gather schoolbooks into pack, placing it by the door before school.
- Vacuum as directed.
- Wash and dry (if it's puddled up) bathroom, kitchen floor once a week.
- Periodic chores such as windows, spring cleaning, yard work as directed.
- Ministry to an elderly or disabled person weekly.

Youth Point Chart 5 (ages 14-18)

– Negative Points		+ Positive Points	
Ignoring Chores or Making a Mess (Including breakfast and sleep schedule, spilling without wiping up, unmade bed, litter, unfinished work, etc.)	- 1 each	**Cleaning Up or Doing Chores Without Being Told** (Includes breakfast and sleep on schedule, taking out trash, brushing teeth, carrying plates to sink, putting things away, helping others work.)	+2 each
Impulse Control Problem (ignoring essential chores, unnecessary anger)	-2 each	**Impulse Control and/or Teamwork** ("I felt like ___, but instead I did this ____ for our benefit", healthy anger management/ problem solving)	+3 each
Softie Love (Not confronting moral situations with unpleasant truth, or lying to escape a moral dilemma)	- 1 each	**Truth in Love** (Telling the truth when it hurts – particularly when it is to your disadvantage)	+2 each
Coercion (I win, you lose; using force or threats)	- 1 each	**Win-win Negotiation** (Let's plan to do ___, taking turns, etc.)	+2 each
Note: Outright Rebellion gets double consequences 1) Immediate down time or spanking and 2) Points off on the chart	-2 each specific instance	**Swift Obedience** (obedience within 3 seconds)	+2 each

continued next page

Youth Point Chart 5 (ages 14-18), continued

– Negative Points		+ Positive Points	
Note: Outright Rebellion gets double consequences 1) Immediate down time or spanking and 2) Points off on the chart	-2 each specific instance	**Win-win Negotiation** (Let's plan to do ___, taking turns, etc.)	+ 2 points
Time-out (lost time for disobedience, Ping Time)	(1 point per lost minute)	**Bonus Points** (given for maintaining a positive total yesterday)	+2 each
Bad Attitude Attack	-2 each	**Fun** – good humor event	+2 each
Negative Points Total	______	Always start out with positive points – these are Grace Points	Grace Points +10
		Positive Points Total	______
		minus	-
		Negative Points Total	______
		Total Reward Points	+/- ______

Again, you have created your own Parents' Expectations Chart. The Point Chart follows (see next page):

Parents' Point Chart 5

– Negative Points		+ Positive Points	
Ignoring Chores or Bad Habit (2-3 essential chores, poor or late breakfast or bedtime)	- 1 each	**Performance of an Essential Chore or Learning a Good Habit** (Complete breakfast and bedtime on schedule, give 5-8 servings of fruits and vegetables to family daily, daily devotional, family sports/exercise.)	+2 each
Impulse Control Problem, or Lapse of Leadership (Lack of planning, ignoring essential chores.)	-2 each	**Impulse Control and/or Leadership** (Using a plan or "I felt like __, but instead I did this __ for our benefit.")	+3 each
Softie Love (Avoiding confrontation of moral problems, allowing inappropriate selfish behavior.)	- 1 each	**Truth in Love** (Confronting and/or stopping selfish, sinful behavior with growth in view.)	+2 each
Ultimatum (Use of force or threats outside the necessary discipline for unsafe or rebellious behavior.)	- 1 each	**Win-win Negotia-tion or Supportive Solution** (creative problem solv-ing or mediation)	+2 each
Out of Balance, Bad Attitude Attack (Lack of mental, spiritual, social, physical growth and balance: hardening of the attitudes.)	- 1 each	**Fun-good Humor Events, Positive Balance** (Dynamic growth and balance of mental, spiri-tual, social, physical activities.)	+ 2 each
		Always start out with positive points – these are Grace Points	Grace Points +10

Parents' Point Chart 5, continued

– Negative Points		+ Positive Points	
Negative Points Total	______	Positive Points Total minus Negative Points Total Total Reward Points	______ – ______ +/- ______

By this time in your child rearing process, your children have ceased to look at you as their primary source of inspiration, and they are reaching out with a "Look out, world, here I come!" attitude.

By the preteen years, your child will have tried those independent wings. He or she will be convinced that he can successfully handle all adult responsibilities. After all, you or the sitcoms have made it look easy.

In other times and places, young teens support families. What kinds of attitude and skill levels are required for them to do that? You can bet that they were trained to set the table by age five, help in the laundry room, garage, yard, and do their share of useful chores to benefit the entire family.

Some of my fondest memories are of "helping" my father with his small building projects, bringing a flat-blade or Phillips-head screwdriver, or a steel tape or other tools as he needed them. We had our heads together on a hot roof or in his workshop, drank gallons of lemonade, and found meaning in making our home a better place to live. I learned about 0000 grade steel wool and the "perversity of inanimate objects"—a term he did not learn in the Navy.

That training was not only painless, it was also useful. I learned a "can do" attitude which enabled me to fix plumbing under the house in sub-zero weather fifteen years later. I was up repairing a tin roof during a storm which blew it partway off and felled a tree in the yard. My experience gave me confidence to keep learning and doing. College testing showed a 98th percentile mechanical and spatial ability.

Was that genetic? I do not think so. Dad was a mechanical engineer. He worked for those skills. I did too. I loved that kind of puzzle because the privilege of working with Dad created in me a thirst for those skills. Work is only a dirty four-letter word when the attitude needs adjusting.

Real world work will give your child enrichment far more useful than you imagine. It will bond you, empower real self-worth, and build social skills and teamwork. I am convinced that when we avoid work we replace healthy fatigue with stress.

How? Ignorance is stress. Ignorance is dependence on any shyster who gives us a smooth scam. Ignorance leads us to feel cheated, victimized, angry and frustrated with good reason. Ignorance is only easy in the short run. When the result of laziness is being fired, fined, frustrated, embarrassed, divorced, or ill, work starts to look valuable.

When youth struts to center stage in an effort to control his whole life and some of yours, you show him the following list of your responsibilities. Maybe you would like to post it and include each section as part of your discipline management and growth effort. There are lots of chores there.

Parents' Duty and Skill List

Does your youth have these adult skills mastered so they can be done fast and well? If not, he remains in a submissive role until he leaves home to establish his own household.

- **Yard and Home Repairs**: Manage workers or repair and maintain yard and home yourself. Paint, build, plan, budget for and buy materials for projects such as roofing, bookshelves, storage areas.
- **Bookkeeping**: Pay bills, keep records of spending, balance bank statements, track credit spending and loan repayments. Plan and carry out insurance and financial strategy.
- **Secretarial**: Do time planning and errands, phone calls, correspondence, special occasion gifts and cards, schedule appoints, games, classes, and special events. Chauffeur people to these events.
- **Files**: Set up and maintain files on all aspects of the household, including financial, warranty, and physical plant information. Keep records on repairs done and specifics of new equipment installed.
- **Protection**: Research, provide for, and maintain the following: inventory of possessions, furniture and valuable paintings. Create and maintain safety rules, fire escape drills, tracking of children away from home, etc.
- **Food Services**: Plan menus, purchase food, prepare meals, serve them and clean up after them. Take into account: nutritional balance, personal preferences, special dietary needs, variety of texture, color and type of food, degree of "cooking," freshness and freedom from unnecessary additives. Food storage rotation and freezer "quickies" for Sunday use must be planned and maintained. Ambiance, service, food preparation and purchase for parties are additional.
- **Purchasing**: Buy toiletries, paper products, small appliances, gifts, clothing, etc. on budget. Wrap and mail gifts as needed.

- **Laundry**: Wash, fold, and iron clothing, bedding and towels, schedule and record items sent out for dry cleaning and laundry, get items from cleaners.
- **Fabric Maintenance**: Mend and perform tailoring on clothing, backpacks, and other fabrics.
- **Physical Plant Maintenance**: General handyman tasks, basic plumbing, wiring, carpentry, and other household upkeep.
- **Daily Cleaning**: General pick-up, make beds; straighten, fold, and put away items, organize magazines, books and newspapers, freshen bathrooms, straighten towels and clean bathroom sink.
- **Trash Disposal**: Empty kitchen, bedroom, bathroom and office trash as needed, recycle coat hangers, plastics, glass and newspapers, prepare trash for weekly pickup.
- **Weekly Cleaning**: Change bed and bath linens weekly, clean shower area, hot tub and shower as needed, wash floors, vacuum and dust.
- **Periodic Maintenance**: Clean windows including skylights and screens at least twice yearly, clean carpets and upholstery, oil furniture with four coats oil inside and out 2 to 3 times per year. Remove books from shelves and vacuum books and shelves. Clean gutters and attic or basement areas.
- **Houseplant Maintenance**: Purchase, repot, water, trim and feed houseplants.
- **Gardening**: Water as needed, use weed killer and spray for insects and diseases. Wash or hose off porches and outdoor furniture.
- **Small Appliance and Computer Repairs**: Schedule and carry out computer virus protection, vacuum and other routine cleaning and repair to prevent

problems before they happen. Record repairs done and by whom.

- **Organization**: Clean out and organize closets, cupboards, drawers and basement and furnace room. Discard out-of-date items, such as spices over six months old or outdated medications.
- **Automobile Repair and Maintenance**: Track oil changes, radiator and belts and regular tune up needs, gas and wash car as needed.
- **Pet Care**: Includes daily brushing, walking, vacation planning and vet visits, shots, licensing and shampoos.
- **Childcare**:
    - Raise children in the discipline and nurture of the Lord.
    - Supervise and instruct them on reasonable chores, safety, expectations and family goals.
    - Teach manners, citizenship, respect for authority and education.
    - Attend school and church events, track homework and project due dates, help with schoolwork, provide quality control of schoolwork and handwriting.
    - Teach and monitor Spelling, History, Math, English, Science, etc.
    - Teach and practice problem-solving skills, negotiation skills, conflict resolution, communication skills, hobbies and anger management skills.

Teach and practice adult skills such as budgeting, spend/save/tithe principles, making decisions, analysis, creativity, synthesis, time management, priority and goal setting, application of right principles, proactivity rather than crisis management, follow through on duties, and interdependence.

You are still essential to your child. It is easy, when children are about 15, for parents to see themselves as more and more useless, obsolete, irrelevant, or perhaps rejected. Extended depression or other dysfunctional attitudes may show up uninvited.

➥ *Stress-free Discipline* helps your child to see you as an honored friend and mentor, a valued part of his life for as long as you both live. The teen years are an important time for teaching your child the more challenging life skills: proactivity and positive balance.

Proactivity

Proactivity is a type of problem-solving behavior with the following characteristics:

- Problems are considered from every possible angle before they become severe.
- Taking positive, preventive, thoughtful action prevents crisis.
- Counsel is sought if the problem is complex.
- History is taken into account.
- Long-term results are positive.

Further, you are responsible for training your children in many life skills. They must understand and be able to analyze the attitudes that lead to passive aggression, depression, suicidal tendencies, underhanded anger and other dysfunctional "bad attitude attacks." The world is complex. Suicide, for example, is epidemic among teenagers to an extent unknown in our history. You can and should teach your children what leads to this drastic action so they can spot and prevent suicide in others.

➥ Public schools teach "life skills" with a variety of textbooks. Read your child's text carefully, and exempt your child from having to learn offensive material. Also read each teacher's class sets of handouts which do not have to go through the usual School Board process of parental review and approval. These are kept in the classroom and do not go home to you at any point.

Positive Balance

Positive balance is key to a healthy life. Begin this phase of parenting by finding what you need to balance your life. Do you define yourself solely as a wife and mother? Father, wage earner, and husband? Do you never extend yourself into the areas that enrich parents after children leave home? Have you given your time so completely to meeting family needs and desires that you do not have any hobbies or get-togethers with friends? Are you physically unfit? Maybe Dad needs a round of golf every Friday afternoon. Has the education you dropped when your family responsibilities got heavy been on your mind? Perhaps it is time for a night class when someone else takes over your chores. Perhaps it is time for community service of some kind. Whatever you choose, the family must "buy into" this new interest as something healthy for you and worthy of their respect. You may need one day off per week for a "mental health day." Where are you on your spiritual journey?

Positive balance is a type of mental, emotional, spiritual and physical focus with the following characteristics:

- It may be active or relatively passive, as long as it:
  - balances a broadened range of interests and activities
  - includes educational, social, healthy, creative, perhaps useful interests
  - uses both right and left sides of your mind[78]
  - causes you to stretch out of your comfort zone
  - brings about positive, therapeutic energy

Take time to consider how realistic your expectations are. Every bad habit takes time to overcome. It is a lot harder to change a bad habit than to simply form a new, good habit, and it takes 32 days to form a good habit. Your child cannot be expected to track all your adult chores, and you cannot do all that positive change at once. Just take your expectations one or two at a time when you present the Parents' Expectations Chart to your child and ask for his help.

The right way, the right time: Children love to help correct their parent's weaknesses. They must, however, do it in a respectful way, at the right time.

- ➥ When we point out our child's weak spots, we must model the diplomacy and grace that God uses with his still, small voice in our souls. A "praise sandwich" works best. Use praise, then correction, then again use praise for the positives. Be specific or it is phony praise.

Cooperation is a skill we wish to foster. Thus we teach a child to diplomatically point out our weaknesses (telling us about them in private) and thank him or her for helping us.[79] Cooperation in this fashion makes discipline easier for the child to understand and accept. Teamwork builds up our relationships. Love adds motivation to mature.

It is easier, then, for the child to eliminate his or her own weaknesses with your diplomatic help. Never embarrass your child by scolding him or her in front of friends. Do, however, pick up your clipboard and pen, or use "the look" (no smile, no whites of the eyes, no words please) with your stopwatch.

Evaluate and Practice Your Teaching Methods

Now that you have reviewed your routine, goals and definitions, consider your teaching methods.

Giving Directions: Practice one skill at a time.

Remember to give instructions for only one thing to do at first. For example, after you have rinsed the diaper in the toilet and squeezed out the water, talking about what you are doing as you do it, then you say, "Jennifer, please put this in the diaper pail." Jennifer will watch, listen, and learn. Once she puts the diaper in the pail and washes her hands just like you do, she will be ready for more complex directions. Next time you will say, "Put this in the diaper pail and wash your hands with soap and water."

Instant consequences and praise work best.

Praise from you and points will please her and be all the reward a small child usually needs. You might add gold stars on a wall chart if you wish, or give out stickers for a job well done. Don't start something you are unwilling to carry through, however.

Give maximum points (as marked on the Point Chart) and voice your praise whenever a chore is done well and completely. Give fewer points for incomplete or poorly done chores.[80] Give those points in silence.

How you give instructions is important.

Have you noticed how good behavior often goes unrewarded in families? What busy parents have time to figure it all out? Let me help you. Never focus your attention on bad behavior.[81] Stress the good result you want to happen. If you say, "Don't touch that!" your child's mind will hear, "Touch that!" Remember to phrase the same idea differently: "Keep your hands off that."

Be sure you're face-to-face, with good eye contact.

Then give one-sentence directives with instructions to come back when your child is finished. In order to get her attention, you may have to put your hand on her shoulder or hold her head close to yours at first.

Have the child repeat the instructions back to you.

If the child immediately "forgets" your instructions, tell him to do the best he can with what he remembers. That way you're not teaching the child to be helpless to get attention. You must never reward "forgetting" what you say by giving the answer. Natural consequences—fewer points—teach more than you know and do not encourage debate or misbehavior.

When the child is successful remembering one task, add a second one.

("Please put this in the diaper pail—hold up one finger as a cue—then wash your hands with soap and water—hold up the second finger.") Have the child repeat the instructions. Demonstrate how to climb up on the stool and wash with soap and water. Then have the child do it. Small children are concrete, literal thinkers. You show and tell first, the child repeats your words and actions back to you. Be gentle, remembering that children only learn abstract ideas later.

Do not scold your child if he forgets something completely. Just say, "No, try again without my help. If you give up, we'll award points and I'll tell you what you forgot."

Never repeat the instructions until after you award points.

"I can't" either means "I don't know how," or "I don't want to." The "I don't know how" part is solved by your posting of each step of the chore.

Giving the child a cue –the next step only –prevents learned helplessness.

For the younger, ignorant child, (non-reading toddler) it's all right to walk him through the motions of the next step only to cue him without using words. Once he can use the VCR, you may want to make a chores tape for him to follow for review.

For older children, "I can't" may mean confusion about the task. For example, in order to explain, you may want to role-play a negotiation. Negotiation can be confusing to some adults. You can have him "act like" his sibling, then find an "I win, you win" solution to the problem.

- If you've interrupted something your child wants to do, it's probably a case of "I don't want to." The "I don't want to" means rebellion and deserves consequences as listed in Section 1.

Handle severe behavior problems.

- In a severe case of bipolar or other acting out behavior, you'll want to make sure the child has appropriate brain chemical balance and follows doctor's orders. Professional counsel is important here. Even in severe circumstances, *Stress-free Discipline* will reduce the stresses that trigger bipolar outbursts. This system is good for every family.

Post each chore/list/expectation.

If you have posted each step of the chore (as I recommend), it is all right for the child to "look it up." Some children are print dependent and some are auditory learners. The auditory learners may find that a tape recording or video tape is a good reference. Since looking it up is a bother, your child will want to master the skill sequence without helps.

Check the job for completeness, then praise and award points.

At that time, you'll give fewer points for incomplete obedience, reminding the child what the original instruction was. Even small credit feels like success. It is a great incentive for your child to do better next time.

After the job is complete, and you have awarded points, give another simple directive. Remember that children need clear, specific instructions. "Clean this up" is not specific enough.[82]

When your child successfully remembers two tasks, add a third one.

("Please put this in the diaper pail—hold up one finger as a cue—then wash your hands with soap and water—hold up two fingers—and come to me—hold up the third finger.") Have the child repeat the instructions. Demonstrate how to climb up on the stool and wash with soap and water. Then have the child do it. Small children are concrete, literal thinkers. You show and tell first, the child repeats your words and actions back to you. Be gentle, remembering that they only learn abstract ideas later.

Learning styles and rates differ.

Remember that there are big differences in how people learn. Never blame or get angry with a slow learner. If you add emotional baggage onto the issue, you will sabotage your child's learning and doing the right things. Some children—even some teenagers—will take a long time to remember two items and do them in sequence—first this, then that. Never show impatience. We are not in a hurry. Haste is more likely to destroy love than to build it.

Award fewer points for incomplete work, but praise all efforts in the right direction.

You might say, "I'm sorry that's not complete; you didn't wash your hands. Do that now. Remember, I asked you to put the diaper in the pail, then wash your hands with soap and water and come to me. But I am so happy you put this in the pail and came to me!

That's 3 points you earned! (Hug, tickle) When you do a complete job, you'll earn more points. Next time I bet you can earn 5 points."

Mid-course correction

...The cheapest road to high quality. If your child asks you—while the chore is in progress—what you would award for points, tell her to guess what might raise her score. This encourages her to analyze what she has done so far. Analysis is a higher order thinking skill which you want to develop. Nod yes or give a "thumbs up" if she guesses correctly. Say, "No, try again," if she is wrong.

Make her work for the points, by looking up the skill sequence you have posted, or by checking a tape to jog her memory.

After success with three directives, give four.

Again, some children will take weeks to do all four things! Praise any step in the right direction, but withhold points when the job is not complete.

After success with four directives, give five.

"Please wash this off in the toilet, squeeze the water out, put it in the diaper pail, wash your hands with soap and water and come to me." Counting on your fingers to emphasize each point will help. Have the child repeat your instructions.

Giving directions at the right time: It is important to respect the child's time up to a point.

Your child will ask you, "What's the big deal about instant obedience when you have interrupted my activity with your orders?" You'll want to time your orders for a good stopping point, in order not to frustrate the child into rebellion (Ephesians 4-5). But you are the judge of the good stopping point. It is best to have chore time at the same time(s) every day.

Be reasonable, but be firm if the child can't find any good stopping point. Don't let a game continue for fifteen minutes beyond the time you asked for obedience. When the child began her game, you told her it would be chores time at a certain hour, and it is her responsibility to track that time. Three minutes is enough time before the "beep" reminds your child that time is passing. Your time is important, and the child must respect it. But again, no debate or negotiation should change your mind once you have decided what's fair. You don't have to justify yourself to your child.

The A-Zone again.

Take two deep breaths and don't let your children see the whites of your eyes. That indicates to them that they won. It's your sign of retreat into your brain stem, the A-Zone, the fight or flight part of you—the adrenalin rush that takes twenty-eight minutes to return to normal. When your eyes bug out, you're ready for reactive, non-thinking action, such as whisking your child out of danger on the street. However, adrenalin does you harm when you need to be coolly writing points or considering the complexities that occasionally arise. Remember, it works against you, since you will not be able to access the part of your brain that contains your education!

Changing the deal is the child's method of controlling you so he won't have to do what you say. Don't change, repeat, discuss, or explain. If you're feeling stupid about your original instruction, apologize occasionally to your child and ask for his forgiveness. Then practice taking two deep breaths before issuing any more orders.

Interruptions

If a child habitually refuses to interrupt her activity when you have given a clear instruction with all the steps listed in Section 1, deep breathing, moving close, eye contact, etc. tell her you will no longer give three minutes to stop what she's doing and obey. Tell her you will give her only one minute. During that minute you are breathing deeply. Then start the stopwatch. The audible beep may remind your child that you are holding her accountable for the time she delays. You don't speak and you don't smile, even when the child smiles winningly at you.[83]

Rebellion

Rather, keep your clipboard handy, where you can jot down the time spent in rebellion. When it reaches 15 minutes (or more if he took off out the door) forcibly interrupt the child at play. Take him home for a spanking. After the spanking you will hug him and tell him how you hate to be forced by his behavior into using this punishment. Then give him 15 minutes (or whatever the time was) of down in bed time or ground him in a chair. Let him know that if he leaves the chair, he will be spanked again.

For down in bed time, be specific: "You lie here quietly with your eyes closed until this timer goes off."[84] He doesn't get his fun until he obeys you.[85] God didn't intend children to have perpetual self-gratification at your expense.

If your child is in grade school, you can tally up the misspent minutes, place them on your chart, and send the child to bed early for the night. Remember, no exceptions, no debate, no changing the deal, no smiles.

Use Stories, Metaphors and Examples to Enrich Concepts Related to Impulse Control

Identify impulse control with definitions; then complete the idea with stories, metaphors and examples. Impulse control is a type of behavior characterized by proactive thinking and by not doing what comes naturally.[86] That is part of the definition. Now you need examples, word pictures, or stories. For example, a person with impulse control problems will slap an infant for crying without solving the problem by finding out what caused the crying. A person who is proactive will solve small problems before they become big. A proactive person will figure out ahead of time when her infant will cry from fatigue or from too much stimulation.

A person who has learned impulse control will look for facts to balance his or her emotional reactions and desires of the moment, suspending judgment and delaying action until later. An impulsive person, on the other hand, will jump to conclusions and leap into action with sudden force and passion. These ideas are characteristics of impulse control and lack of it.

What are some examples? A child with impulse control will be able to play in the sandbox without throwing sand or poking a playmate with the shovel. A word picture might be someone who starts the race before the starting gun is fired.

Analyze your own impulse control: Children will bring out the best and the worst in us, and we have to deal with our own impulse control problems in order to train them out of theirs. Do we react without thinking, making poor choices? Do we let bad habits control us, rather than confront and change them, with professional help if necessary? Our little gifts from God will mimic our every move, for better or worse.

Establish Good Work Habits

Good Routines

Keep a routine time when you expect routine chores to be done. An after-school snack, conversation with you and then chores provides a good physical and mental break from stresses at school.

Promote Teamwork

Until you arrive at Point Chart 3, award points for teamwork under Impulse Control.[87] Remember that teamwork does not just mean that one child cooperates with the other in playing a game. If one child habitually submits to the other, you'll want to arrange your awarding of points to include the idea that both must win equally. Another idea is to alternate leadership and follower positions. Leadership practice starts here.

This might mean that your children share the TV remote control every half hour, or schedule mutually acceptable games by alternating playing dolls then trucks, for example.[88] It might mean they both give up their activity of the moment to play a third game.

Success in today's world requires the ability to cooperate and negotiate, as well as to subordinate one's own desires to the needs of others. These skills take years to learn. *Stress-free Discipline* builds on skills from one chart to the next in order to encourage problem-solving skills and produce intelligent, responsible adults.

Structure the child's work time

Remove distractions like games, TV, and friends. The fun does not happen until the work is done. When the work is done, give free time without interruption for a while. This means you will need to be proactive. Think through what you want to accomplish for the day with your child. Have a goal in mind for each day.

Work with the small child in the same room; don't expect him to do the work without you there as you begin training. A very young child is not capable of self-directed activity when you're not there. As he grows, earning more and more points for impulse control and obedience, he will become more and more competent by himself.

Hone your communication style

A strong-willed child needs you to be careful in your communication style.[89] If you say, "Do your homework or else no TV," your strong-willed child will choose disobedience just to watch you dance around the remote with your eyes bugged out. The better way to phrase your instruction is, "Feel free to watch television after your homework is done."

The strong-willed child will need to be aware of consequences before the event. He also needs you to carry through on consequences, to be fair and not to reward him for bad behavior.

Do the hardest stuff first

Do most of the work when you're both reasonably fresh. If you need a snack and emotional break before chores, recognize this. Then do chores and reward yourself with rest and relaxation time afterward—even if it's only 10 minutes. You can ask your child to help you with pre-preparation of dinner in the morning, alternating play and work time throughout the day. While school age children need unwinding time after school, food preparation may be just what they need after your hug of greeting.

Television will not connect you with your child, and will shorten her attention span, so don't let her talk you into letting her "relax with it" right after school. Start children setting the table, making the dessert and tearing salad, and let them snack during work time. Fruit and vegetables are very good for raising blood sugar and mood without spoiling a child's appetite for dinner. Sugar or fat-laden snacks and soda pop fill his body with empty calories that do not build body cells or energy the way fruits, vegetables, nuts and seeds do.

Be proactive: Think ahead.

Recall that time spent in shopping, putting away groceries, and meal preparation takes 20 hours per week for a family of three (without special homemade recipes). Therefore, if you want more quality time to make both you and your child feel loved, you must plan ahead. Keep a shopping list handy, preferably one preprinted for basics so you don't even have to write on it. There are many books on effective housekeeping to cut your chores short.

Remember that four minutes spent in planning saves up to twelve minutes in doing. Four hours spent in planning saves up to twelve hours in doing. Efficient planning will cut months off your chore life and add time to your fun life.

Use *Once A Month Cooking* to get 30 day's worth of entrees in your freezer with two days of effort.[90] All the repetitive chores, like washing your pots and pans 30 times, are then eliminated. You'll be baking five chickens at once, using pans and washing up only once, rather than repeating the cooking and washing up (time-wasting motions) on different days.

➥ Reread this text often.

Discuss items that do not make sense with your spouse, learning partner or with someone whose experience and judgment have been well proven. Remember, however, to choose your mentor by the fruit of their work and similarity of experiences to yours. For example, if your ADHD child is a concern, consult with someone who knows ADHD behavior and lifestyle, discipline and treatment.

Remember also that until you have tried this system for 32 days, adhering carefully to the instructions, you need to stay with this program without modifying it. Chances are you'll be advised by someone unfamiliar with *Stress-free Discipline* principles that they are unworkable. That's not true. Dr. Jones has revolutionized school discipline and your child's teacher may be more familiar with his process than other professionals. Bottom line: this works.

➥ Use the Boy Scout rule: If the child is able to do it himself, even if it's not a perfect job, make him do it himself.

Don't even think of doing it for him. If he messes up the job, award incomplete points. When you have walked him completely through the specifics of the chore, he knows what to do. He can use a cue list he has made, if he is a teenager.

Students from grade six on up ought to have their own Day-Timer. Grades five and six are the most difficult ones for most children: the danger zones which create dropouts. A Day-Timer which you check will help them succeed.

The Oops! Disease—kill it before it multiplies. If your teaching is fuzzy, your child's job will be incomplete. In that case, feel free to apologize for your fuzzy communication and teach the job over. Don't erase the negative points!

➥ That's right. It's your child's job to make the task clear by repeating the directions and asking questions until he or she understands the job from beginning to end. If she doesn't pay attention to the details of the job, she's partly responsible for the communication problem. You are preparing her for dealing with fuzzy communication from an employer some day in the future. If she doesn't have the habit of clarifying instructions, she'll get in trouble for "not following directions" on the job.

➥ **Rewards**: At each stage of accomplishment, award points and praise. Thanks, hugs, healthy snacks and tickles are good additional rewards beyond the points. I would not connect them with the points, but if you are using another rewards system, mesh it with this one if it fits. Children hate change.

Make one mark for each point, crossing four marks with a fifth, so the child will learn math concepts while earning points. If you've begun a sequence of instructions with a teenager, he may not want a hug, but a playful touch on the arm may be a good substitute.

The Rewards Ceremony: Your child is further rewarded with quality time spent in educational activities with you. Dad, you must be available for this as well as Mother. One night a week of family time is the minimum. Let children choose the educational game for their awards time, as long as parents approve...and parents for theirs if you desire. All activities must be educational and personally interactive. No fair sitting down to a TV program or any "solitary independent play" like children in a sandbox.

Build Self-confidence Through Excellence and Growth

Real Praise is Specific

Parents, your praise should be enthusiastic for every step your child takes on the journey to a complete job. You might say, "All right! You remembered to do lots—first three, then four things! You're pretty smart!" Specific, real praise sets up the child's expectations that he can really do the jobs, and do them completely. Success with simple chores like this will transfer to an attitude of "I can do it" when he meets new challenges.

Help your child build higher order thinking skills.

After you have put your Parents' Charts into practice, if you've cut down from eight cigarettes per day to four per day, you'll get points on impulse control from your son—the one who's been hiding your cigarettes or flushing them down the toilet. He will love you for this. This process brings your child into higher levels of thinking: first application, then analysis, and then judgment.

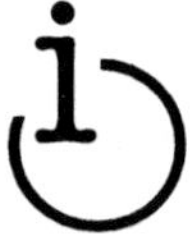

True self-worth avoids many pitfalls: When the child can physically do the job, he or she is given the chore, thus developing realistic self-esteem. Being waited on teaches helplessness and—most importantly—denies the child a true sense of self-worth.

Unrealistically high self-esteem is just as bad as very low self-esteem. Ironically, antisocial criminals have high levels of self-confidence, allowing them to justify abusing others.[91] When a person feels better than others, unrestrained pride leads to destructive, "playing God" behavior.

Realistic self-worth will not only relieve you of stress, but also build respect for you as the child meets your needs along with his own.[92] Do not hesitate to ask for help from your child. Every child searches for meaning, identity, and approval from his parent. Service to parents thus builds a sense of meaningful, worthwhile personhood in your child.

Some parents proudly assert that they would not ask for help from their children, even when they are in severe need of help. They feel that their status is somehow diminished in the eyes of their child...perhaps they fear rejection. Aged, hurting parents will maintain this stance.

➥ Be assured that when we ask for reasonable help from our children, we build love, not disrespect.

They are happy to return to us some of the service we have given so freely to them. We just want to be careful how we ask. We do not wish to be excessive or demanding about this. Thus, we practice being independent whenever possible, but admit when we are overwhelmed. Men, trust me, this gets easier with practice.

Full Respect with Quality Control

Remember: do not award full points for half a job. The highest positive points represent a top job—well done. A job that is not well done and complete should receive fewer points. However, never award more than the negative points listed in the minus column. (Most of these negative points are deliberately made lower than the positive points, so the child will end up with more positive than negative points. Success breeds success.)

Award Points Daily or Weekly or Every Hour or Two, Whatever Works Best

Reinforce the idea that when your child helps you, there is more time to do what you both want. The Points System shows this daily, since not meeting standards denies your child something he wants. The point system also keeps you out of your right brain feelings and emotions, and forces your thinking into left brain discipline mode.

Discipline Priorities

Whenever the child is misbehaving and the parent has "pinged" him by pushing the stopwatch button on him, this issue takes priority over everything else. Other activities need to stop until this issue is finished—until points are awarded, and writing on the parent's clipboard is finished. If a child has "pinged" her parent, for example, for shouting (impulse control problem) or for repeating a command, that issue comes second to the child's misbehavior.

➥ Agree that only one person will allow himself the luxury of being angry at a time.

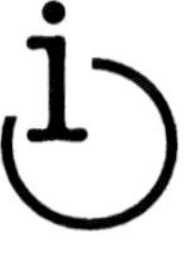

Remember deep breathing. Stretch. Get over it. Keep your goat on a tight leash. Remind each other to take deep breaths. Snap a rubber band on your wrist every time you begin to lose your temper. Withdraw for a short time to pray and read the Bible. Give each other twenty-eight minutes of space for leaving the A-Zone if this is practical. Minimize conversation. Use images to convey feelings, and "I" messages to relate feelings. For example, "I feel angry when you do not come to the dinner table the first time I call you. Food gets cold, and I can't enjoy myself."

Avoid Hostile Accusations

"You don't ______________________" only creates stronger anger, rebellion and defensiveness.

Down time for rebellion: Keep that list of deliberately disobeyed commands at the back of your clipboard. It is part of the daily summing up. Bring it out when you impose early bedtime, restriction of privileges such as game time, TV time, "free time" or time with friends, etc. Remember that negative points caused by rebellion are "down time," and may involve sitting on a chair in the corner or other frustrations for the child. During "down time," set a kitchen timer out of reach of the child (but in view) to help her see how much time she has left to serve. Ignore what she says, sweet or nasty. If she jumps off the chair, it's a spanking and resetting the clock.

Remember, when the choice is between frustrating your child or frustrating yourself, do frustrate the child. The more strongly the child fights against discipline, the more it is needed now rather than later.

➥ Jail time is a harsh result of lax parenting, and the parent who fails to train a child to control his impulses pays greatly in the long run. Military school costs $21,000 per year, with therapy costs on top of that.

Even failure to teach a child to enjoy reading can lead to discipline problems, so remember to make reading together, in a book of the child's choice, part of your rewards program.[93] Also read together when it's not a specific reward. Reading increases attention span and focus, even reading aloud.

Just kidding? Not likely: Occasionally a child will claim, "I was just kidding," when in fact he was lying. Lying is intentional deception and it is a hostile act. Take points off for harsh "kidding" under Impulse Control.

Points on Points

You'll have to add points to the charts several times in a day. Keep charts with you on a clipboard.[94] Copy the original blank charts so you can have a clean chart on your clipboard for each child each day. You may want to laminate the charts and use erasable marking pens on them. Give your child a clipboard with your charts on it as soon as he or she can read. Keep a daily total on your calendar.

It's better for you to review the child's point chart without brothers and sisters there. An audience is never a good thing during discipline. Naturally you'll want both children to give you their own version of what happened, but there's less bickering if each child gives his or her version in private.

If a disagreement arises over something you did not see, the best policy is to punish both children with negative points, since they will both justify their own behavior and you'll never get the whole story. This is easily done, especially if you have chosen group management and rewards.

If it seems to you that the negative points aren't enough punishment for the crime, you may want to catch the offender in all the negatives you can find for other problems to make sure they don't feel rewarded for their own cleverness. Don't change the negative points on the chart. Just be ever-present and aware.

➥ Never subtract negative points from the next day's reward time if you give daily rewards. The same is true of weekly reward time. Every beginning is a new chance.

Strong-willed children seem to misbehave more when they are punished. It takes them longer to accept discipline. Thus you will find that you'll want to "catch your child being good." Praise will give the added love and assurance—incentives to be good—which is probably what your child needs when misbehaving. Soon your child will remind you of his worthy point-getting behavior if you overlook it. Make sure it is verifiable so your child won't be tempted to lie to "pad the account."

Use Motivational Games for Reward Time

These should last for the number of minutes that equal positive points earned (minus all the negatives). When the minutes are up, the game is put away. It is not available except for reward time.

> ➥ A very short game will inspire your child to behave better next time. There should never be so many negative points that a game is not played at all. That's why the positive points for right behavior outweigh the negative points for failure. Special time with you that is tied to performance will be a bigger motivation than you can imagine.

This event should have emotional and educational merit, and should include conversation and treats. Educational merit includes teaching social skills, such as how to eat a special meal together, or it could involve remembering a set of objects in a picture. ("Look at this photo for 30 seconds, then tell me what things in it you remember, one point—base or move—for every object.") It should not be a movie, electronic game or other non-personal interaction. Some possibilities are below.

Educational Baseball

Try a game of educational or just plain "baseball" (in your living room if the weather is bad) with other children in your playgroup or family. A stopwatch or countdown timer helps speed up a slow game if memory or flash cards are part of the game. Allow three seconds for a response, and then the player is off base into the dugout.

Educational baseball uses flash cards: Consider this if your child has vocabulary words or math facts to learn. It might be a game with a scripture where you gradually subtract words (an erasable white board is ideal for this). Correct answers move the player from first base to home base, from first to second, and so on. You may choose to give unlimited tries until a wrong answer (or two or three) makes the child go to the dugout.

Memory Baseball

"Just plain" baseball will move a smaller child along the bases without requiring as much academic competition. It might involve memory questions like, "What did I serve for dinner yesterday?" It might involve judgment questions, like "What is your favorite color?" The idea is not to stump the child, but to make the questions hard enough to require some thought and attention to detail. Cause and effect questions are also good.

Strategy Games

Chess or dominoes can increase your child's attention span, math, spatial and strategic thinking skills. "Risk" will help your child predict events and plan for them. It is all right to leave a game in the middle, continuing it at the next rewards time.

Kinesthetic Games

Adapt other games, such as Nerf basketball, to be used with flash cards. One person, the coach, calls out a word part from the flash card or the master list, and the team members get to shoot a basket (or several until they score a point) when they remember the definition. (Competition and performance should not be part of these games until the child has become competent in memorizing the flash cards...just play for fun before then. If your child despises competition or feels self-conscious you may wish to modify the game. You know your child best.)

Check out a teacher supply store. Shop with the children and respect their veto. If they do not like anything you like, ask them to invent an educational game. This will force them into advanced thinking skills such as analysis, synthesis, and judgment.

Performance Games

Enjoy Drama and Literature: create our own skits. You might consider taking a TV or novel plot and reforming the characters and the plot as committed Christians rather than godless opportunists. How would someone with a true relationship with Christ react to frustration, fear, disaster, etc. You might even do this with Bible characters. Did Cain have a good relationship with God? He got angry when he was corrected and got into deeper trouble with God. If he had told God he was sorry and had followed the rules, would things have come out better? How? Try also imposing real world consequences on the shallow fantasies which end so comfortably for selfish TV characters. What risks do TV characters take when they do what feels good at the moment?

Improvised Games

Act out a book or story, adding your own words to put a twist into the plot. Each right answer can allow the child to determine what happens to familiar characters, and the game can go on until the time limit expires. To encourage and reward creativity, let the child create and act out part of the plot of an original story. You begin the story by prompting the child to define two or three characters (at least one good guy and one villain), a time and a place. Specify that it has to involve "realistic" events and forces.

Add Complex Puzzles as Motivators

You're the only judge when it comes to throwing down a challenge to your child's understanding. You want the child to be interested and engaged in the process, perhaps complaining and squirming, but you do not want to go beyond a reasonable frustration level!

If she bursts into tears or he stomps out of the room, you have gone too far! Be sensitive and loving, no matter what the outcome.

When it's your turn, add complications or frustrations for the good guy. When your child uses easy "quick fix" solutions to the problem (as in "kill the bad guy"), say, "Is that the best way to solve the problem?" or "Suppose the bad guy is an unsaved friend?" or "Is that legal?" Explore choices to see which one causes the best long-term positive results.

Avoid Easy Fixes

Some alternate possibilities to violence or science fiction "easy fixes" include court-ordered mediation, compromise that does not hurt the good guy (win-win solutions), "time-out" for the villain, social sanctions, and isolation of incorrigibles. Children may create a punishment for the villain based on early bedtime or no snacks.

Help the child to make the punishment fit the crime

Help your little one to think about the consequences of the rule-breaker on others. Television shows rarely show these! Then ask what seems fair. When the child gives an answer, respect that answer. Then you may want to diplomatically point out some options, or just leave space for change to come about naturally.

Explore "what if" ideas

Encourage your child to explore punishments based on a study of sociology or history. He may be too young to make judgments, but as his knowledge and maturity grow, he can learn enough about history and sociology to develop those higher-order thinking skills. Thus, he will reinforce lessons learned in school.

Check his history book

After you recover from the shock at what's left out, you will be able to analyze together what is put in.[95] First, he must be able to recall facts and then apply them with your help. This exploration together makes your time fun. It also raises his grades in one of the hardest school subjects.

Ask your child, "What worked in that culture?" and "How severe does a punishment have to be in order to change everyone's behavior?" Some people require less punishment than others before they will conform to society's rules. However, rules are for everyone. Historically, fewer rules or laws are necessary when a strong ethical community base exists.

Remind your child that in order to live well, we must consider the long-term effects of a punishment. For example, one remote Alaskan village imposed life alone on an island on a villager who committed murder. This punishment seems severe, but is based on the principle that rules plus relationship equal cooperation. In a close community, everyone knew the punishment in advance, and assumed that people were responsible for controlling their own feelings. As a result, murder was generally unheard of in their community. On the other hand, someone who cannot control his or her temper might have community service as a discipline.

Explore the differences with your child between discipline and punishment. Define cruel and unusual punishment. Defining the words we use, especially "love," will give you much to discuss.[96] Is discipline always unquestioning control? What would Jesus do?

Early Native American tribes punished drunkenness by tying the hung-over person to a tree and letting everyone who wished to whip him. Modern answers to that problem involve a psychologist coaching the person's relatives, teachers and employer. They are taught how to impose boundaries and consequences on a problem drinker. These consequences will come into a drunk's life if he or she fails to attend AA or fails to stay clean. Appropriate proscriptions, shame and pain—emotional or physical—often prevent or minimize repeat offenses.

As the hero (or heroine) of a fictional story solves problems, the child learns problem-solving skills. It's useful for children to know that all people at all times of history have had to solve problems like these.[97]

If your child is very shy or introverted, and perhaps hates games, just reading to him or her is a special treat. Perhaps your child hates competition. Many books on the market have non-competitive games in them. Choose to learn some new games, adapting them with your time needs in mind.

Musical Metaphors

Musical metaphors—stories set to music—can teach many concepts. 🕮 *Mind, Music, and Imagery*, by Stephanie Merritt, Aslan Press, 1996, has lists of musical works useful for educational activities, memory, creative writing, exercise, sleep, and therapy of various kinds. You will want to read with discernment, since the book is not biblically based. However, a great deal of useful information is contained in it. Chapter four has interesting neuro-biological information indicating that the wrong music (incessant rock) can cause difficulties in learning and memory.

Role Playing

Incentives may include playing "You be the parent" with your child, to see if the child can give points and monitor you doing two, three, and then four things. This type of game is a good reward for points earned. It also teaches interdependence, which will be a joy as the child grows in competence. Provide dress up clothing, hats, and other props for this imaginative play.

Improving Attention Span

Reading increases attention span, raises I.Q., and nurtures higher order thinking skills such as analysis, synthesis and evaluation.[98] Children remember the lessons of the little engine that could, the narcissistic dog that fell into the pond, and other stories which show consequences.

These readings are especially fun if you get over your fear of being ridiculous and dramatize the story. Teenagers learn consequences as they read about the tragic flaws of characters in classical literature. Bad choices are lived out in the imagination, rather than in real life. Experiment with changing the choices of the main character, and changing the endings. Take turns reading and dramatizing the story with older children.

The Appendix includes activities that will increase your child's thinking skills (brain builders). Coincidentally, these learning activities are also the incentives you can use to "connect" with your child in lifelong bonds of learning and the excitement of discovery.

After years of frustration in schools, it's easy for adults to forget that learning is fun: a reward in itself. Do not wait until the school teaches higher order thinking skills. Your child's thinking ability can be seriously retarded by then. These skills take more individualized attention than your child's teacher may have time to give.

For these reasons I urge you toward family reading time and other educational activities to improve attention span. Larger cities have teacher supply stores with a wide variety of games and materials for all kinds of interactive quality time spent with your children. Ask your child's school for enrichment materials and they will give you sources.

➥ You may ask, "Why does it matter if TV and electronic games shorten a child's attention span?" Here's why. Being able to make wise choices depends absolutely on being able to maintain focus while delaying action until more facts are known. Then one must delay action again until facts have been evaluated... using some kind of historic, cultural and ethical context.

Research, critical thinking and logical reasoning are skills that require time, effort and dialogue. A short attention span shortens this long process, making it ineffective. The media presents a false logic, where images presented together lead to assumptions of—for example—cause and effect where no such relationship exists. God had good reasons for not giving us the Bible on DVD.

People who depend on the media are constantly misled. Any comparison of the script of a TV show with the actual show will demonstrate this to you. The scripts present mere skeletons of an argument. Images provide false logic to give the impression that something logical and reasonable has been said. Complete presentations of facts are not popular with our ever more illiterate audiences. Just realize that parenting is the most difficult thing you will ever do. There are no short cuts to rational thinking.

Success Is Biblical, Reasoned Choices

Success is proactive behavior: thinking ahead[99]

Reasoned choices must be learned and practiced over and over. If your child always chooses the "fast food" of short-range thinking he will not have the solid nourishment of reason. If he specializes in following his feelings he'll not be proactive in a crisis. He will never have practiced making choices based on careful evaluation.[100]

Suppose your daughter chooses fast fun over slow disciplined thinking when it comes to her love life? She's in for pregnancy when she is not ready for parenting. If she lives with a man before she marries him, she has a 75% chance of struggling through the trials and failures of single parenthood. If she marries a second time, her changes for success are even lower than those of a first marriage.

Do you see where this lazy thinking style of sound-byte logic leads? It leads to a serious disability: lack of concentration leads to accepting the flashy and the comfortable over what's reasonable—over what has worked for centuries.

Are we adults always looking for an easy life without any effort—pleasures without our sacrifice of time and energy? That's not realistic. There is no free lunch. There is always a price to be paid. Mature adults learn to enjoy the price. The process of earning our pleasures becomes a pleasure. That is why family teamwork is so important. It's modeling real world, joyous living.

Success in reaching worthwhile goals brings happiness: Happiness depends upon two basics—matching our skills to our tasks, and adjusting our goals and our desires to fit reality.

Let us be thinking Christians: Bereans. I pray that we will have the courage to submit all to the control of Christ as we run the good race. Where is fast fun and lazy thinking—entertainment and immediate gratification—in that picture? Let us be slaves to Christ rather than to our own sin, and let us train our children in the disciplines of responsible adulthood.[101]

➥ **A word about television and electronic games:** "The average American adult watches (TV) a shocking 26-30 hours a week, or about four hours a day.... This dependence puts your health at risk. It increases your chances for weight gain, reduces your problem-solving ability, and cheats your personal relationships. This may be television's greatest threat to your health. It allows you to block out difficult feelings (stress or anxiety, for example) while encouraging you to skip the activities (like talking to loved ones or engaging in hobbies) that can help you resolve tough feelings, gain a sense of accomplishment, or otherwise grow and develop."[102] Electronic games are also junk food for the mind. They both substitute for healthy life skill development. That lack of mental and physical skill- and relationship-building threatens you, your children and your family as a whole. Try www.familyfun.com for economical ideas for family activities.

The best success in life is love (1 Corinthians 14:1a, 1 Corinthians 13:3, Matthew 22:37-40). Our love is how God will evaluate us. See Matthew 25:40. The best expression of love is time (1 John 3:18, Ephesians 5:2, John 3:16a). The best time to love is now (Galatians 6:10, Ephesians 5:16, Proverbs 3:27). Have I made a case for restricting your family television or video game time? I hope so. You might want to put that on your chores chart, so your child can help wean you away from the soaps or the sitcoms. If you're tired after work, nap for 20 minutes or take a shower to refresh. Then connect with your children. Have them read you a story.

Your Family Vision Is Essential for Building a Strong Family!

What is the Purpose of Your Family?

- (To be read out loud in a quiet place...with feeling): Is family a place where, when we knock, they have to let us in? A resource? A refuge? A learning center? A millstone, touchstone, milestone, bulwark?
- Is family a burden, a standard, a fortress, something you pass by on your way to personal fulfillment? Is it a source of enrichment?
- Is family a labor force which produces leisure for us? A safety valve for venting? A nuisance? A service organization? An embarrassment?
- Is family a critical, negative, no grow force? A hostile communication environment? A place where nobody cares? A bad example? A lost childhood? A fragile identity? A den of thieves?
- Is family a sense of roots? Is family something we use and abuse? Is it security in the midst of our adventures? A fantasy? A team? A sacred duty? A place to go when we are old and broken? A warrior-priesthood band of brothers?
- Is family a survivors program? A listening post? A source of bragging rights? Who, on their deathbed, ever said, "I wish I had spent more time at the office?"
- What's the point of having your family?

Here is the Challenge

- Provide one copy of the Family Vision for each member of your family.

- When you each read the above list, add anything you each feel your family represents to you right now if it is not on this list.

- Separately from other family members, without discussion, circle or highlight five terms from above or from your list to represent where you feel your family is now.

- In red, circle five terms which express where you would like your family to be a year from now. Let the red signify Christ's blood for you, because His forgiveness and grace is the only thing which will empower you to build your family up. Will power—and guilt when you fail—alone do not work for long.

- Share your vision with your family members and create a consensus of where you want your family to go from here.

Section IV

Questions and Answers

How do I play a game when I have three children and one has to stop early?

If you're playing a team game, send the rebellious one with fewer positive points to bed early (or grounded to a room devoid of entertainment) and change the game to one which is easily played with just two children. Your laughter will impress the bed-bound child with a determination to behave better next time so he can stay up. If the rebellious behavior does not stop, consider giving everyone positive points for each hour or two your child can control himself. We want to increase the odds for our rebel to get positive attention from you and from siblings.

The stopwatch seems like a great tool, but I'm afraid I've overused it.[103]

Overuse of the stopwatch may turn it from an enjoyable tool into an emotion-laden penalty. *Stress-free Discipline* works best by preventing problems before you must use the stopwatch to enforce time-out. Your proactive use of no-smiles, in-the-face, clear instructions should help children know you mean to supervise and enforce your directions.

Ask yourself: Is my instruction fuzzy? Did I walk my child through every step of the process I am asking him to manage? Am I speaking deliberately but kindly, with "I mean it" body language or have I slipped up there? Have I "changed the deal," allowing my child to escape negative points for sloppy or unfinished work? If you have changed the deal, apologize for your mistake and get back on track. Take your negative points on your own Chores Chart for leadership failure. Don't worry. Children love it when you're human and honest with them. God's not finished with any of us.

Just remember that your child can't grow when boundaries keep moving according to your mood, even though he gets juvenile pleasure out of getting his (or her) own way. Do not change the deal. Quality control at home prepares your child for the demands of work and school.

follow-through: Overuse of the stopwatch may mean you're weak in follow-through checking of the work done, with instant praise and recording of points. Your need to use the stopwatch often (meaning that poor childish choices are happening more often rather than less often) means that the rest of your program is weak. Add follow-through to your parents' expectations, and have your child "ping" you on it when you forget.

Review and practice the other parts of the program, preferably with a friend or learning partner who thinks differently than you do. Without ongoing feedback and friendly reminders, your good intentions will easily degrade into bad timing and reactive emotions.

➥ Never use time to manage a behavior that you can manage with your presence. Record yourself, if necessary, to see how you sound and whether your voice is calm, focused and clear—don't holler from the other room.

Then stay with any child who needs you in close range in order to "remember" what the task is. You may need to put your hand on a shoulder or turn a small body in the right direction to get the job done. You may want to kiss, kid and tickle to encourage the child, but do not let the child turn aside from the task at hand.

Practice, practice, practice doing the task until the child can do it without you there to point out how and where the child should move. Then be sure to follow up with points, so good behavior is reinforced. If you fail on this step, poor behavior will follow, not one time but many times for your single lapse of attention. Remember that you must award points every single time a job is done.

Prayer with your child over your issues is a must. And remember, God will not zap you with instant follow-through or any other skill. We have to work through it with His help, but He's guiding the ship and we're responsible for the forward movement.

Boundaries: Often our children not only recognize their own desire for power, but also their need for boundaries. They need us to be strong leaders, but they also need our understanding, and we need their help. Yes! The whole family needs wisdom from above, the kind which is "first pure, then peace-loving, consid-erate, submissive, full of mercy and good fruit, impartial and sincere. Peacemakers who sow in peace raise a harvest of righteousness" (James 3:17-18).

Peace is...Remember that you will be blessed when you are a peacemaker, but peace is not an armed truce or temporary cease-fire. It is a creative, nutrient force that has confronted sin and problems and has resolved them in the victory of Christ. True peace allows everyone to grow in goodness.

As parents we need to ask ourselves: What do I have to know, do and be in order to resolve this issue? Often the answers involve time and effort, changes and sacrifices we may not want to face. I have to know this system thoroughly, follow through on scoring points consistently. I must be patient, investing time now to create good will and family teamwork later—when the dust settles and this is routine. I must learn biblical precepts as well as the precepts given here. I must model submission to God's will and be open enough to be honest with my children when I fail. Resolve to do the whole system, or do not expect results.

It seems my breathing is the first thing to "go south" when something happens. How can I solve this?

Every morning set your alarm for 15 minutes before getting up time, and focus on your breathing. Set a book on your abdomen and focus on continuous, even breathing while imagining a difficult event in progress. Do this exercise again at night as you're falling asleep. As you relive negative events of your day in your imagination, practice slow, deep belly breathing. Use deep breathing during the day when you notice yourself tensing up.

Stretch your whole body in the midst of stress, thus relaxing your muscles as you remind yourself sternly to "Breathe!"[104]

My child still doesn't clean up the bathroom without being told every single step every time. He's thirteen years old and of normal intelligence.

Probably he got away without doing the cleanup once, and must be repeatedly supervised. Even one lapse of attention on your part results in your child trying your system over and over and over in hopes of another escape from responsibility. Just be consistent in using the system.

My children are constantly at each other's throats. I'm always involved in being the umpire or the judge.

It's normal for brothers and sisters to compete for your attention. Keep to the *Stress-free Discipline* program with one addition. Spend at least two hours per week with each child separately from the others. Have a picnic, play a game, go out to the library or to an event or to a pancake house for breakfast. Let each child know through your focus on his or her interests that he or she is a special individual. Realize that as your child receives recognition for the good he is doing, sibling rivalry will evaporate.

Parents can mediate arguments by setting fair, written ground rules, such as no name calling, stay seated during the discussion, no interruptions of the speaker. Define the issue by restating what each person says. Brainstorm solutions, then see if children can agree on one solution. If there is no resolution, go back to brainstorming. It may take some time, but this process can help them resolve their own conflicts in the future.

Also, consider teaching children to compromise. Rules for common activities can avoid trouble. Game nights may help children consider their sibling as a teammate.

My anger is just uncontrollable no matter how hard I try to stay cool.

This is probably the greatest challenge we have. Our little angels know every angle to use in order to trigger us, distract us, and thwart our best intentions.[105] We become frustrated by our failures and want to give up.

When our child goads us into a response by saying, "I hate you," or "I'm going to run away," or "I'll call Child Protective Services," or "You're just mean," we make the big mistake. We answer back. As Dr. Fred Jones says, "Open mouth, slit throat."

Depression, an American epidemic, is usually caused by anger. We have different anger management styles, and if anger is a long-term, severe problem, we need to find out our style and work through incidents with a good counselor. Nagging, our second nature as parents is prompted by underground anger. We think we're not angry, just concerned, we say. In fact, we're pressured by our past, our busyness, our peers, our finances, our fears, our pride, disappointments and our complex physical ups and downs. We lack the mentors and models and skills to grow mentally and spiritually. We are ashamed of our lack of control over our own feelings. We're going nowhere, but we're getting there fast.

> Remember that anger is the physical result of pain, frustration, or fear. It is triggered by unsolved problems and unresolved issues.

God wants those issues to be brought into submission to a godly worldview. Maybe that's why He gave us children! How many of us would subdue our anger if our children did not point our weakness out to us? Aren't they the greatest catalysts for change in our lives? We need their insights. They need our ability to be real with them. We both need to realize our spiritual infancy.

Triggers: If we could just prevent that triggered response which causes us to blow up! One solution is to ask your child to carry a stopwatch and start it on you when you deviate from the discipline plan! This forces the child from his or her right brain (the feelings/anger part) into the left brain (thinking), automatically moving one of you out of the anger danger zone. Ask your child to punch the button any time he sees you flare-up with words, with set jaw, or with the whites of your eyes showing more than normal. At that point, you have forgotten your two deep breaths and have "lost it." He can make a mark on your discipline chart whenever rage gets the better of you.

It's scary to put that kind of power in the hands of a child! What's to keep your child from punching the stopwatch unfairly in a fit of anger? Answer: nothing, except your calm talk about anger beforehand.

When your child punches a stopwatch unfairly on you, it's past time to define terms. Before this happens, talk about anger. What is it? Whose anger is it when the stopwatch is triggered? Helping your child define and recognize anger is especially important if you have ignored your own anger signals long enough to be unaware of them. Draw angry faces: the brows knit together, the eyes narrow, the mouth turns down, the lower lip sticks out, and the head is thrust forward. Remember that we said the "I mean it" face has no expression—neither frown nor smile.

You are asking your child to hold a mirror up to your angry face when she punches the stopwatch on you. She is your feedback tool to improve your discipline technique. Your child's honest sense of what's fair will win over a temporary anger fit. If the child is wrong, she will model your behavior when you're wrong. Do you erase incorrect points? Ask forgiveness when you make a mistake?

Children often have well-developed "hypocrisy detectors." If you smile with your mouth but not with your eyes, this sends up a "red flag" to children. They sense when the body language does not fit the words. They know—often subconsciously—when something's phony. Play a game of "What's phony?" with them to help them learn to identify feelings as they really are. Body language is the truth when words are a lie. Look for a "body sentence"—several gestures which mean the same thing. Growing up involves you teaching children how to identify and deal with negative feelings. Anger is key among these.

Any child will love this game of correcting your discipline style...and games are great learning tools for growing both of you.

- Finish your day with "I love you more than," a game you can play with your children as they are going to bed. "I love you more than sunshine on roses," gives the child a word picture that may mean more to her than simply saying "I love you."

"How can I instruct my child without teaching her to play helpless in order to get me to do the task for her?"

The only sure thing about learning is that we will forget. How, then, do we "help" when it is really needed? There are three parts to the best helping interaction:

Praise what has been done right so far.

Prompt by telling the next step: only the next step.

Leave, say no more and turn back to your work.

Appendices

APPENDIX A

Personality Analysis

Severe problems are caused when we fail to do the work of appreciating individual differences. People actually get divorced over differences in personality and thinking styles. However, God designed personality differences knowing they would stress us. He expects us to submit to each other in love (see Ephesians 4 and 5). Why, then, do we insist that people around us be our clones? Why do we try to remake our spouse and children in our own image? Why do we argue until doomsday about small issues? Why do we fight over who is right rather than consult an expert? Why do we choose friends who are exactly like us, blinding ourselves to people who can enrich us?

God designed personality differences in order to eliminate our blind spots, to enhance our problem-solving ability, to add depth to our vision, spice to our lives, and different skill sets to our life's work. Embracing differences and respecting another's point of view is work for most of us. But it is time to step out of our comfort zone (the boat) and set foot on the stormy sea of the unknown if we want to follow Christ.

As parents in a fast-lane world, we can use the following worksheets to identify our own strengths and weaknesses. From that vantage point we can understand what vicious cycles result from personality differences in our family. Usually Mom and Dad have different styles and goals for their parenting, and that's the first conflict that needs to go. Consistent discipline requires conscious agreement between parents.

Once we know our own strengths, we'll probably find that our spouses have opposite strengths, perhaps to an extreme degree! Remember, we are to submit to one another in love, and speak the truth in love. Successful, stress-free parenting requires mutual respect and clarity—both partners must be slaves to Christ, and team players as parents. Strong-willed parents pulling in opposite directions create a rotten witness to their children, who will take the first opportunity to reject the faith of their parents.

Personality Profile and Preferences

Ideally, a counseling professional administers the Myers-Briggs personality profile. What we're doing here is an "informal assessment"—an educated guess. There is no wrong answer. For your convenience, I have extracted benchmark information (under sections I – IV) from 🕮 *The Art of Speed-Reading People* by Tieger and Barron-Tieger, 1998. Commentary is mine.

Each set of traits (in boldface) has many small preferences that, together, show that you lean toward behavior on the left side of the page or the right.

Place your initial near the preference that usually shows how you behave. Read and do this very quickly. Your first response is what we want.

If the preference is strong, place your initial very close to the left or right item. If you seem to express both preferences, place your initial in the middle. When you finish a set, see where your initials indicate you usually behave. Consider how you are usually energized, for example: by being with the outer world or being by yourself? When you are by yourself, are you usually lonely, sluggish, restless and unmotivated? Are you energized when you are with people? You are an extrovert.

As you progress, choose one of each boldfaced pair as your preferred mode of acting (example: are you an extrovert or introvert? A sensor or intuitive?) At the end of this survey you will have four letters that show a single personality (example: ENFP).

To be consistent, an extrovert will not have too many introverted preferences, or if he/she does, they will be moderate, the result of conditioning, and will disappear under stress. The opposite area will show weaknesses. An extrovert, for example, who prefers interaction with people, will be unhappier, less energized when alone.

Stress and conflict result from playing a role unsuited to your personality type. However, knowing your weak areas can help you train yourself into skill and grace.

When you understand your own lifestyle, you will see how you can respect and love others who are different. They complete you. They are not in competition.

Some personality types find discipline of themselves and their children easier than others. If discipline is harder for you, realize that this is a weakness which must be overcome regardless of your personal preferences. You will need to be outside your comfort zone if you want the good results of consistency.

Overall, more extreme expressions of a strength or weakness will create stronger life drama and change, but a person who is predominately in the middle of the continuum will experience serious internal conflicts. Seeing both sides of an issue is an advantage in some situations, a disadvantage in others. How do you make and respond to your choices?

How People Are Energized

Place the initial of your first name on a spot on each continuum to show how extreme or moderately you show this trait. Bear in mind that you will have an overall personality on one side or the other of each boldfaced pair of traits that follow.

1	2	3	4	5	6	7	8	9	10

Where do you fall in this spectrum?

Extrovert (E) (the outer world)	1|2|3|4|5|6|7|8|9|10	**Introvert (N)** (inner world)
Interacting with people		Being by oneself
Focuses energy in outer world (people and things)		Inner world (ideas/thoughts)
Works on several projects at once, global		Single-minded, linear
More comfortable acting first than thinking at it		Steady proactive, details first
Public/dominating the conversation person		A private person
Comfortable w/letting others really getting to know him		Values privacy/secretive
Interrupts and finishes other people's sentences		Talks more slowly, usually more quietly
Easily distracted		Focuses attention on one subject at a time

Now look back on your individual choices, and determine which side of the page best expresses your personality. Repeat this exercise with your mate in mind. Then do it again with the child who most frustrates you. Then continue with the next sets of traits.

Time spent on this will give you the kind of insights that will relax you when you apply *Stress-free Discipline*.

As you explore these ideas, respect personality differences. It is utterly useless to try to remake your introverted child into an extrovert. Your child may make his or her own modifications, but it's not your job to change a child's personality. For example, you won't succeed in making your dreamy idealist into a goal-driven, type A personality if that's not how he or she is designed by our Creator! If you try you will only frustrate everyone and stunt your child's growth.

Stress-free Discipline is designed to relieve you of judgment-driven conflicts based on personality differences. It is also designed to work harmony within personality differences. Dreamy children must still function in the competitive world marketplace of the 21st century.

Your task, then, is to persistently teach the skills necessary for success without destroying the love bond between you and your child. An introverted child need not have a huge, frenetic birthday party. A quiet activity with one or two others might be better than pushing team sports or noisy competitions. If you are an extrovert, your respect for an introverted child will gain you his lifelong loyalty.

The Kind of Information We Naturally Pay Attention To:

This represents the greatest difference between people, the greatest source of conflict and (if likes are paired) causes serious blind spots in problem solving.

1	2	3	4	5	6	7	8	9	10

Where do you fall in this spectrum?

Sensing (S) (65% of the population)	1|2|3|4|5|6|7|8|9|10	**Intuition (N)** (35% of the population)
Sees the trees		Sees the forest
Seeks facts, details		Seeks connections, implications, underlying meaning
Down to earth, sensible		Imaginative, creative, intuitive leaps
Awesome detail memory		Forgets where the keys are: detail is a bother
Trusts experience, data		Trusts instinct, needs less proof it will work
Prefers practical utility		Prefers new ideas, theories, concepts, hypotheses
"Gets things done"		"Thinks things up, weak follow-through"
Enjoys setting up systems, following procedures, efficiency		Avoids routine for long periods
Uncomplicated, precise sentences		Complicated, circuitous communication style
Short, one thought sentences		Long, rambling, even unfinished sentences
"Just the facts"		Uses many analogies, metaphors, repeats thoughts w/different spin

Do you see serious areas of conflict? These conflicts can strip discipline of all effectiveness, and can be the kind of "red herring" which draws everyone off the parenting track.

Perhaps you are a person who hates routine and is always inventing a new parenting scheme. You are weak on follow-through, and can't spit out a simple, precise sentence to save your soul. How does this personality trait impact your children? You ramble and forget the end of your long, complex sentence which was brilliantly studded with linguistic flights of fancy. The children cannot sort through the verbal circus to find out what to do. You're confusing them with three ways to do the dishes.

Your impatience with consistent, simple routine must be modified if you want family harmony and discipline. Just like healthy eating, healthy discipline is routine. It is also restful and efficient. At the same time, it is repulsive drudgery to some of us. It is necessary drudgery. Decide to do it.

Suppose you are a parent who immediately trusts a detailed, proven discipline system, but your spouse appears to sabotage your efforts by being experimental. You are practical, sensible, and efficient. Your spouse never repeats an effective routine. Rather she is happy with her imaginative, motivational adventures with the children. The children love it. You're the bad guy. Effective routine is forgotten despite your best efforts. Divorces have centered on this type of conflict. Now you see why we're doing this exercise.

Choose your battles. Laugh about it. Your spouse may never feel comfortable with detail and routine. Work together to agree on nonessentials: The beef stew doesn't have to be made the same way every time. Beds do not have to be made the same way every time.

Morals, health, safety, and discipline have to be done the same way every time. Each team member illuminates blind spots in others. More importantly, we each compensate for the weakness of others. Christians call it grace.

How We Make Rational Decisions (by what criteria):

We may have such opposites in our families that we often miscommunicate.

1	2	3	4	5	6	7	8	9	10

Where do you fall in this spectrum?

Thinking (T) (Principles)	1|2|3|4|5|6|7|8|9|10	**Feeling (F)** (Values)
Uses objective pros and cons		Considers effects on self and others, what's right
Logical and analytical		Empathetic, sensitive
Depersonalizes language and decisions		Personalizes issues, language, choices
Truthful even when it hurts		Tactful, even if stretching the truth
Able to confront		Anxious in confronting; will tell half-truths, avoid confrontations
Most persuaded by logic		Most are persuaded by emotional appeal
Applies standards fairly despite consequences		Mercy and harmony over justice
May be blunt, argue for fun		Diplomatic, gentle, avoids arguments
Appears low-key and matter-of-fact		May appear excited, emotional
Usually very assertive		May lack assertivenes

Notice how each personality trait has advantages and disadvantages, depending on the wisdom of when and how it is used. For example, being argumentative and cool or distant is an advantage in some situations, but a disadvantage in others.

The civilizing process involves impulse control, a major part of *Stress-free Discipline*. Know that "expressing ourselves" can be worse than useless if we do it at the wrong time or place. This is where we need to be aware, asking God for wisdom. We need to train our children, since we are the ones translating the world for them. They need to know that "expressing their personality" or "letting it all hang out" often means rehearsing their errors, making errors habitual. It often makes problems worse, delays healing, and builds walls between people.

Imagine you have no trouble being truthful, despite the emotional consequences on your children, but your wife gets upset. Facts are logical and objective—your comfort zone. Sometimes you get too blunt, or the timing is bad, but you feel unmoved by your "oversensitive" wife and children. Why can they not be more like you? She can't even assert the truth when discipline depends on it. *Stress-free Discipline* helps her overcome this weakness without battles. You have to get more sensitive. Blunt arguments destroy your love bank deposits. Practice grace in everything which is not a moral, health or safety issue.

- Separate facts from feelings. Do not indulge in "right fights." Facts can be verified with data or expert input. Feelings must be honored as emotional reality. Agree on a counselor and then consider agreement on binding arbitration by that counselor for serious issues.

How We Like to Organize Our World, Live Our Lives

1	2	3	4	5	6	7	8	9	10

Where do you fall in this spectrum?

Judging (J) (Planning it)	1|2|3|4|5|6|7|8|9|10	**Perceiving (P)** (Winging it)
Make a quick plan and stick to it		O.K. with changing plans, collecting more data
Natural respect for authority, hierarchy		Questions/rebels against rules, restrictions
Must be in control		Comfortable letting others control
Productivity very important		Process as good as product
Generally very organized		Trouble finding things, organizing
Must finish work before relaxing, often workaholic		Procrastinates, takes mental health time
Formal, conventional, traditional		Unconventional, casual, non-traditional
Less harried, unhurried		Often frantic, frazzled
Answers questions quickly, often without asking clarifying questions		Delays offering opinions, usually asks more questions
Adamant, confident answers		Tentative, equivocal, modifies positions a lot
Driven to finish one project before starting another		Concurrent projects
"Filers"		"Pilers"

At this point, you can look back over these charts and notice where the stressful differences lie. If you happen to be a "filer" and your child is a "piler," it is appropriate for you to require your child to learn the skills needed to create files. As an adult, every minute she spends filing will save her four to twelve minutes, perhaps days, searching for misplaced paperwork. Every hour spent planning saves four to twelve hours in the doing.

If your child is a perceiver, her strength is also her weakness! The time a "Judger" will save by planning ahead will leave him or her refreshed with creative, mental health time in the end (if he will take it). The perceiver child will have unfinished projects everywhere, may change goals as the project unfolds, and will appear frazzled, messy, irreverent and focused on fun. If the perceiver is your spouse, he will be late to the airport every time.

The perceiver's approach only works where there is no deadline, safety, health or moral issue at stake. Help this family member know when to be firm, when flexible. Work together on plans and priorities, write them down, and reward yourselves when they are complete.

You can remind your "piling" child that she probably doesn't enjoy searching for stuff as much as other activities she can name. She must master this skill.

Perhaps, on the other hand, you are the one who needs your systems-oriented child to "ping" you for leaving important tax-related paperwork, bills, insurance paperwork, etc. lying around loose. How many days would it take to find old receipts if you were audited?

Notice that there are advantages to traditions and ritual. Ask your irreverent child to build family rituals to unify and build the family team. Explore the advantages in time saved by doing a task the same way every time, thus cutting hours off your chore time. Getting creative about washing windows just prolongs the process.

Creativity can be a curse if it is used in random, explosive fashion, regardless of where it is appropriate. If creativity and nontraditional approaches are part of your child's personality, find ways to express that personality as part of the team and not as the rebel. Be open to concurrent house cleaning projects, even if the shambles does not come together into order until the end of the day. You see how the process works. You can be proactive in order to relieve each family member of stress which up until now has been a dreadful routine.

Opposites attract because—ideally—they are designed by God to balance each other. Give personality differences to Jesus in prayer. He wants us to express love and to do it with "sound mind"—whole brain—balanced thinking.

Also, ask yourself: Am I a strong-willed individual who will make a federal case out of every little concession my spouse asks of me? Test yourself with the following information gleaned from a Focus On the Family radio interview with Cynthia Tobias, author of 🕮 *You Can't Make Me (But I Can Be Persuaded)*, 🕮 *The Way They Learn*, and 🕮 *Every Child Can Succeed.*

We annoy each other because we're all different. Something happens when a strong-willed person is added to the mix, even in a strong Christian home, creating incredible rebellion, defiance, disobedience and harsh attitudes. You correct and change the behavior, but you need the strong will if you are to progress. Thomas Edison, Albert Einstein, Madame Curie, and many others were strong-willed children.

We need to teach the child through love, respect, and understanding to do the right thing without all the power struggles and anger. The enemy doesn't want this book in your hands.

Are you highly strong-willed? How many times is this true of you?

A Strong-willed Individual...

- almost never accepts words like impossible, crazy
- can move fast from being loving to being a cold immovable force
- when bored, can create a crisis
- considers rules to be more like guidelines
- shows great creativity and resourcefulness
- seems always to find a way to accomplish the goal
- before this person will do something, it has to matter personally, not "supposed to"

- negotiates before compliance can take small issues and blow them up into huge ones

  ➥ Strong will is not a negative trait, but is attached to some of the most successful, compassionate, energetic people.

Never let strong-willed children get by with special favors: they should not have trouble with authority and boundaries. They struggle instead with how the authority is communicated. Outwardly they can be easy to get along with, but the "or else" is one of their favorite paths. You can't force them to do anything. You don't have to do anything except die, and a strong-willed child may choose to die over eating peas.

It's your job as parents to teach, hold accountable, not let them get by with bad behavior, but it's not your job to force people. He never did. You can insist on high standards, enforce rules, but you can't force people not to take the consequence. How you speak to a child makes all the difference in the world.

Stop yelling at the strong-willed child: the effect is alienation (no leverage). As a policeman, you can't give a lecture and a ticket to a violator. We give too few tickets and too many warnings as parents. If you don't have a relationship with your child that they want to keep, you have no influence.

APPENDIX B

The Stress-busting Technique of Deep Breathing

The following quotes are taken from 🕮 *Natural Detoxification* by Jacqueline Krohn, M.D. and Frances Taylor, M.A. Hartley and Marks, Publishers, 2000. ISBN 0-88179-187-3. Pages 341-342.

> "The more air we move in and out of our lungs, the healthier we are. The efficient functioning of all our body systems is determined to a great extent by the delivery of oxygen and removal of carbon dioxide. Deep breathing can balance the functions of the entire body, including respiration, circulation, metabolism, digestion, elimination and glandular function. The body cannot cleanse itself, heal itself, or maintain life without the oxygen supplied by breathing. Deep, easy and full movement of breath allows relaxation, and increased oxygenation can produce spontaneous emotional release.
>
> "Breathing also affects the circulation of lymph. The motions of respiration mechanically pump lymphatic fluid through the body. If breathing is restricted, fluid builds up, causing edema and the build-up of waste products from cellular metabolism. Detoxification cannot take place efficiently if lymph circulation is impaired.

"Breathing is the only function of the body that we can perform both consciously and unconsciously. Many illnesses and health problems arise from an imbalance of the autonomic nervous system. By working with the breath, we can positively affect the autonomic nervous system and many of its involuntary functions.

"Breathing is also directly connected to our emotions.... Our emotional state affects the speed, depth, regularity and noise level at which we breathe. Breathing slowly, deeply, quietly and regularly can calm anger. Clearing anger by changing breathing constitutes an emotional cleansing. In addition, the physical after-effects of anger, such as headache and an increase in blood pressure are prevented. Negative emotions, such as nervousness and impatience, can also be helped by full breathing."

In his book 🕮 *Natural Health, Natural Medicine*, Dr. Andrew Weil recommends the following simple exercise to relieve anxiety, stress and emotional upset.

Sit with your back straight.

- Place the tip of your tongue against the ridge of tissue behind your upper front teeth. Keep your tongue there during the entire exercise.
- Exhale completely through your mouth. You will make a noise as you do so.
- Close your mouth and inhale quietly through your nose to a count of four.
- Hold your breath for a count of seven.
- Exhale completely through your mouth to a count of eight, making a noise as you do so. This is one cycle. Repeat the cycle three more times, for a total of four complete breaths.

Begin by doing this exercise twice a day. As you become accustomed to it, you cannot do it too frequently. Always keep the count ratio at 4:7:8, regardless of the speed at which you are counting.

You might notice a shift in awareness or consciousness after four breaths. This is a sign that you are affecting your involuntary nervous system. The breathing exercise is a tool that is always available whenever you need it. Use it to help you in stressful situations, and to help you fall asleep.

Effects of Poor Breathing on Allergies and Environmental Illness:

Dr. L. M. McEwen of London, England, reports that many people with environmental illness suffer from dysventilation (poor breathing), in which breathing is shallow and rapid. Some of the most incapacitating symptoms experienced by these people are caused by the chronic cerebral lactic acidosis (an excess of lactic acid in the brain) that results from dysventilation. Once this pattern of breathing is established, it becomes self-perpetuating.

Food and chemical allergies as well as candidiasis can contribute to dysventilation, and asthmatics frequently have this breathing problem. Dysventilation encourages histamine release by the alterations it causes in the immune system. Learning appropriate breathing techniques can speed the recovery of many environmentally sensitive people."

APPENDIX C

The Importance of Acid-Alkaline Balance

> Some behavior problems in children are caused by an unbalanced biochemistry.

Dr. Krohn and others have much to say about the pH balance of the body. Dark field microscopy of live blood activity shows an intense drama being played in our bodies when our blood pH balance is upset. The factors in our blood that allow us to have healthy enzyme activity, absorb minerals, and fight off pathogens are changed drastically by pH imbalance. We are faced with potential life or death issues when we ignore this vital balance.

Again I quote from 📖 *Natural Detoxification*, by Kron and Taylor, pages 235-238.

> "The body functions through a series of biochemical reactions involving acids and alkalis, which control many body processes. An acid-alkaline balance is essential to the proper function of the body. An imbalance is toxic and causes many adverse symptoms...The measure of whether a substance is acidic or alkaline (basic) is expressed as its pH. The pH scale ranges from 0 to 14. The neutral point is 7; all

values below 7 are acidic, and those above 7 are alkaline or basic.

"Acid-alkali reactions are necessary to the biochemistry of the body, and unless they occur at the proper speed and in proportion, the body can develop an acid-alkaline imbalance...considered a toxin, since the body cannot function properly and can be damaged.

"The pH of different parts of the body is crucial to proper digestion.... Imbalance in the blood, for example, can cause nervousness, hyperventilation, seizures, sore muscles, chronic indigestion, menstrual problems, hard dry stools, abnormal glucose combustion, dissolution of bone, kidney, liver and adrenal disorders, obesity, fatigue and headaches, and feelings of stress, anger and fear. Excessive production of lactic acid during severe exercise or hypoxia (a deficiency of oxygen reaching the tissues) also produces metabolic imbalance...."

Have I now convinced you to go to your nearest druggist for pH testing strips (about six to fifteen dollars)? Note also that various medications change your body pH and require remedial action on your part.

Easy Testing for Biochemical Imbalance

(from Dr. John Walsh, Anchorage, Alaska, 1999):

The best time to measure pH is two hours after breakfast, for several days.

Interpretation	SALIVA pH	URINE pH
IDEAL	pH 7.0-7.5	pH 7.0-7.5
MARGINAL	pH 6.5	pH 6.0-6.5
High risk for acidemia	pH 6.0 or less	pH 5.5 or less
ACIDEMIA	pH 5.5 or less	pH 4.5 or less
High risk for alkalemia	pH 8.0 or higher	pH 8.0 or higher

Methods of Raising the Body's pH:

- Cultured dairy products: yogurt, buttermilk, and cottage cheese.
- Citric acid: Two tablespoons lemon juice morning and evening in water on an empty stomach.
- Balancing free, ionized calcium with bound calcium.
- Supplementing in people with adequate calcium levels with potassium citrate (1 tsp. three times per day for one week).
- Ridding the body of acidic substances, such as ketone bodies, aspirin, alcohol and certain drugs monitored using the anion gap.
- Ridding the body of unwanted sources of oxidative catalysts, such as mercury and excess iron.
- Countering inflammation.

Notes about pH and Calcium:

NEUTRAL pH CALCIUM: CA gluconate and orotate (a good bone builder) need to be taken when proper average pH balance is reached. The average pH is found as follows: saliva pH x 2 + urine pH ÷ 3.

ACID CALCIUM: CA lactate is acid producing, useful if one has a high average pH or urine and saliva (7.0 or above), and wishes to bring it down.

ALKALINE CA: CA Citrate, Hydroxide and Carbonate may cause pH to be too alkaline. It is OK to use if the average pH is 5.8 (acid urine and saliva) and you're working to push it up!

➥ Remember to return to neutral calcium forms when proper pH zone is reached.

APPENDIX D

About Spanking

Go to Family.org to search for spanking links and articles. Consider buying 🕮 *The New Dare to Discipline*, by Dr. James Dobson. Ask for a free booklet called "Questions Parents have About Discipline." It covers subjects like how to set limits, corporal punishment, and developmentally appropriate discipline. Also recommended is a monthly packet of games and sequential age-related parenting tips and newsletter "Focus on Your Child." Learn about this at focusonyourchild.com or write Focus on the Family, Colorado Springs, CO 80995. Phone: (800) 232-6459.

APPENDIX E

Problem-solving Matrix

Ask yourself these questions:

1. What is the problem? Define it precisely. Here's a sample definition format: Running a red light is a type of behavior problem with the following characteristics. The person who disobeys traffic rules may get a ticket, kill or hurt someone. Use this definition exercise often with your children. The more they can work out consequences, the better able they will be to make choices independent of you.
2. Whose problem is it? If not yours, ask yourself what power you have to bring about a resolution. Ask also whether this problem ought to be high on your priority list to solve.
3. Consider causes.
   - What are the causes of this problem?
   - Are these true causes?
   - Assume they are not the causes; what else might be considered a cause?

4. What are possible solutions? Brainstorm these, and then throw out the least practical ones.
5. What results do you want? What is a godly solution? Pray for guidance and wisdom. Test all your possible solutions:
    - It must preserve what?
    - It must accomplish what?
    - It must avoid what?
6. List tasks that must be accomplished in order to bring about my solution.
7. What are the human/equipment resources I need to bring about my solution? Cost? Location? What do I have to know, do and be in order to solve this?
8. Prioritize tasks and put a time beside each. Expect that each task will take from 20% to 100% more time than you anticipate.
9. Map out tasks on a timeline, with deadlines and resources listed for each task. Which tasks may be done concurrently? What is the deadline for the entire project to be done? Make a calendar plan, backing up from the final deadline date to the present. The tasks should be broken down to weekly goals.
10. Group tasks according to skills/equipment needed. Who will supervise the doing of each group of tasks?
11. Pray for guidance and help from God. Then go to it, knowing that He who began a good work in you will see it through to a successful end. Complete the following:
    - Could we modify something we already have?
    - Should we add something? More time, greater frequency?
    - How can we make it stronger, higher, longer, or thicker?
    - What should we duplicate, multiply, exaggerate?

APPENDIX F

Getting the Most Work for the Least Effort Through Prioritizing

> This idea earned an efficiency expert $25,000 from Charles Schwab, President of U.S. Steel: "Do the most important thing first, and keep doing it until you are finished or can go no further. Then do the next most important thing."

Even if you only get work done on two priorities, they will increase your effectiveness about 80%.

A simple priority system for you and your child might look like this (see top of next page).

TASK LIST	GOD'S PRIORITY	LONG-TERM IMPORTANCE	URGENCY URGENCY	TOTAL POINTS	PRIORITY LIST
	(Up to 30)	(Up to 10)	(Up to 10)	(Per row)	(Numbered)
1. Plan Schedule	20	10	6	36	2
2. Food Management	20	6	2	28	3
3. Pray, Study Bible	30	10	2	42	1
4. Spend B'day money	1	3	10	14	4
5. Transport Children, to Work on Time	5	3	3	11	5

Finding the most important thing to do first:

- List important tasks on the left side of your paper.
- Make five small columns to the right of the list.
- In them, give the task a number from 1 to 10, with 10 being the most important.[106]

It works like this:

- Assign points to each column for each task.
- If you're weak there and really working on planning and scheduling, you may want to assign points for that job like this: (A) God's priority – 20, (B) Important long-term – 10, (C) Urgent this week – 6, (D) Total points – 36. Leave the priority column blank until the end.
- If you have food management well organized, have plenty in the refrigerator and pantry, and can throw together healthy meals without much effort, you might assign it points like this: (A) God's priority – 20, (B) Important long-term – 6, (C) Urgent this week – 2, (D) Total points – 28.
- If you want God to be Number One in your life, your day is ruined if you're not up early to meet

with Him, you'll probably give that points like this: (A) God's priority – 30 (B) Important long-term – 10, (C) Urgent this week – 2 (D) Total points – 42.

- Spending birthday money doesn't look so important now, but you have a burning desire to get to the store while the sale is still on. Those points might be (A) God's priority – 1, (B) Important long-term – 3, (C) Urgent this week – 10, (D) Total points – 14.
- Suppose that the children have no tests or major school events today, and you have flex time at work—no hurry there. Taking children to school and getting to work might earn points like this: (A) God's priority – 5 , (B) Important long-term – 3, (C) Urgent this week – 3, (D) Total points – 11.
- You will now write in the priority column: Number 1, do it without fail. Meet with God, 42 points.
- Number 2 with 36 points is planning and scheduling. Do it next. Number 3 task is food manage-ment. That's essential and doable. Number 4 task: Oops, spending birthday money looks more important (14 points) than getting the children to school and you to work (11 points)! Maybe your feelings got ahead of what's right in the circumstance. You decide to get the day's work done, get the children to school, and take a long lunch hour to go to the sale.

If you find yourself overwhelmed, it is probably because you have not prioritized your daily life. A great deal of what we consider essential to do today is the less import but urgent small stuff. The long-term important things get pushed out of the way. Then, when they become a crisis, we go into a tailspin of frenzy, stopping everything else to take care of them. Is this how you wish to live?

APPENDIX G

Brain-builders Step By Step

Whether you are working with a pre-school child or a teenager, every idea or concept—simple or complex—begins with recall of facts.

Step 1: Recall

In order to develop this thinking skill, teachers use activities related to the following:

- Look at books, tapes, charts, newspapers, magazines, diagrams, records, models, people, films, television, radio
- Then show, explain, locate, demonstrate, recognize, discover, restate, identify, inquire, match, illustrate.

For example: Using a children's book, look at a page and see if you can identify anything red—or round—or covered with fur, etc.

Step 2: Application

- Every higher concept must go through steps 1 and 2 before going on.
- Look at this diary, scrapbook, photograph, collection of objects, stitchery, cartoon, map, mobile, model, sculpture, illustration.
- See if you can organize similar objects together, apply a code to the puzzle, construct something like it, sketch it, paint or draw it, solve it, choose something in the kitchen like it, and experiment with it.

For example, look at this collection of tools, and see if you can circle the ones which belong in our garage.

Step 3: Analysis (taking apart the known)

- Make a graph, survey, questionnaire, commercial, report, diagram, or chart.
- In order to do that you will have to categorize, take the data apart, sorting and classifying, dissect, analyze, separate, compare, contrast and describe.

For example, in order to create a graph of the side effects suffered by grandfather because of his fourteen different medications, you will have to take each medication separately listing the side effects by category, then compare side effects by checking off the ones your grandfather has. One young lady recently confronted her grandfather's doctor with a graph listing the medication names on the top line, the side effects down the left side, and the problems her grandfather suffered in each cell of the spreadsheet. Out of twelve medications, grandfather had dizziness, insomnia, constipation, and nausea caused by eight of the medications.

Step 4: Synthesis (putting together the new)

This requires Steps 1, 2, and 3, and then one can...

- Consider a story, poem, play, pantomime, news article, cartoon, new game, invention, radio show, product, recipe, magazine, puppet show...
- And add to it, create, imagine, combine, plan, suppose, modify, predict, hypothesize, design, invent, explain, infer, improve, compose or originate a product from this.

For example, taking a recipe for pancakes, modify it to make muffins.

Step 5: Evaluation (judging the outcome)

- Looking at an editorial, a panel evaluation, court trial, self-evaluation survey,
- Justify, debate, solve, recommend, judge, criticize, consider, weigh, appraise.

For example, using steps 1-4 and the rubric provided for your teacher for this project, decide what grade you should receive.

APPENDIX H

Teaching Tips for Preschool Children

Under Age 1

Yes, you can discipline a baby: you can interrupt his feeding time for breast biting or throwing food. (Not for more than a minute or two.) Rather than saying, "No" all the time, be specific: "Keep hands off the plant." For hitting or poking you can demonstrate soft touch, rewarding with smiles and praise.

➥ You can remove him from temptation. Distraction and challenge are your best tools.

A toddler's misbehavior usually stems from being tired, hungry, or bored. It's easy, though, to over-stimulate the baby's sensitive nervous system with loud music, or by playing long games which demand focus or fine motor skills he may strain in learning. "Baby Sign" language is a good communication tool. Praise calmness rather than rewarding tantrums. Time-out may include being put in the playpen without toys and left there if you determine that the child is not misbehaving because she is ill, wet, bored or hungry. Rebellion earns time-out.

Age 3 and Below

Usually by three you have taught your child colors, beginning to count objects, rhymes, songs and shapes. A three-year-old can imitate you, if you give one brief direction at a time. Provide "dress-ups" if you want to play "You be the parent." Use literal, simple stories. Symbolism is far too complex. Be brief. Always use the same words for special chores you want done. Sharing and taking turns are hard to do. Listen at eye level with the child. Help each child to succeed at something.

Age 4

Favorite words are "How," "Why" and "What." Attention span is still short. Ages four to six are eager helpers. These children, though, may defy you with unacceptable behavior just to find out what your limits are. Emphasize that actions have consequences every time, and you control your actions (impulse control). Use large teaching pictures to reinforce basic concepts. You can find books, for example, which teach manners, recognition of feelings, and basics of going to the doctor, doing chores, playing fair. Montessori materials use touch, sight, smell and taste to teach ideas. You will want to follow this pattern. Bragging and boasting is common. Do not be shocked if you see your children engaged in spitting contests or other similar games. Give each child a chance to "lead" by serving a snack, holding a picture, etc. Structure time with other children; have your child participate in group activities.

Age 5

Your child still thinks literally. He may sight-read simple words, recognize tints or shades of common colors, recall short Bible verses, write his name clearly without help, talk accurately about recent events. Avoid comparing your child with others (a good policy at any age). Explore and dramatize. Girls are maturing more rapidly than boys: do not worry. He can play for quite a while cooperatively with one or two friends. Your five or six-year-old child can also feed the pet, get dressed, set the table, put toys away, put clean clothes in drawers and dirty clothes in the hamper.

Age 6

Your child will still be eager to help. This is a good time to begin moral training with in-depth discussion of why an act is wrong. You will still need to watch that you do not talk too much. The child will probably be in "concept overload" if you use complex sentences. Keep instruction to three simple sentences.

Ages seven to ten are good ages to be more structured. These children can take out garbage, empty the dishwasher, help prepare meals, clean floors and walkways, fold laundry, walk the dog, dust or polish furniture. Nine or ten-year-olds can wash, dry, and put away dishes, vacuum, help bathe the dog, use the washer or dryer, water the yard or houseplants, straighten up rooms, etc. They need clear structure with stricter penalties than younger children. These include withholding privileges, etc.

APPENDIX I

How Do I Know When My Child Has Mastered the Chart?

Mastery is measured by what you accept for consecutive correct responses. If your child does the task three times fast and well, exactly as you instructed, do you accept that as mastery? At some point there is no point in continuing to teach technique. That point is mastery. One hundred percent correct performance is the goal of such a parent. After all, we would not want our surgeons or air traffic controllers to settle for a 90% safety rate. Not all parents want this standard, however.

People who like to think in terms of academic measurements may prefer approximately 90 percent of the total possible points for your Child's Expectations List. You decide your standards; you know your child best. Here is one possibility which gives maximum time for reward (see next page):

	Cleaning Up (Item #1) + Doing Chores	Impulse Control	Healthy Break-fast and Bed	Truth In Love; Truth Telling	Swift to Obey	Win-Win Negotiation
Mastery Level, Children's Point Chart #1 100 average points per day	70	20	10			
Children's Point Chart # 2 160 average points per day	70	20	10	40		
Children's Point Chart #3 201 average points per day	81	20		20		
Children's Point Chart #4 206 average points per day	102	20		20	40	24
Children's Point Chart #5 321 average points per day	204	20		20	40	32

APPENDIX J

Use Music at 60 Beats Per Minute (No Words!)

Music has been shown to lower stress levels, promote healing, increase learning and memory retention, stimulate creativity and imagination, renew and enrich life. It is used in Europe to accelerate learning and has been researched and used here as well. The best is done when our hearts are at 60 beats per minute. Because our heart's rhythm tends to match that of the music we hear, research shows that music with 60 beats per minute and no words is the best music to learn by. If the same music you have learned with is played during a test on the same material, you will do better on the test!

Music has been shown to decrease neurotic disorders when combined with learning activities. When children are feeling angry, hyperactive or aggressive, music can calm them down. Dr. Alfred Tomatis, a French physician, believes that music energizes the brain as well. I list a few selections for different purposes taken from the book, 🕮 *Mind, Music, and Imagery* by Stephanie Merritt, a San Diego psychotherapist.[107] If you choose to buy this book, you will want to review it with a discerning eye in regard to New Age assumptions.

For Calming Hyperactive Children

Try Massenet's "Dimanche Soir" from Scenes Alsaciennes. Aggressive hyperactive children might benefit from a march, followed by Vivaldi or Telemann flute concertos. J.S. Bach's Brandenburg Concertos, Arioso from Cantata No. 156, and Air on a G String vie with Brahms Violin Concerto (second movement) and his "Lullaby" for effectiveness. Introspective types benefit from Impressionistic music, such as Debussy or Respighi. Handel's "Water Music," Pachelbel's Canon in D and Mozart's "Concerto for Flute and Harp" are also good ideas. Watch your child's reactions to your selections to determine which ones work best. Haydn's Cello "Concerto in C major" (second movement) and Mendelssohn's "On Wings of Song" are also good. Begin with Brandenburg Concertos or "The Four Seasons" to match high energy, then throttle back to slower, calmer music.

All Children Will Benefit From...

...Light uplifting music like "On the Trail," by Grofe from the Grand Canyon Suite, or "Flight of the Bumblebee" by Rimsky-Korsakov. Be sure to include Symphony No. 101, "The Clock," by Haydn and Mozart's "Eine Kleine Nachtmusik."

For Children In Utero and Infancy

Try J.S. Bach's flute Sonatas, Beethoven's Piano Concerto No. 5 (second movement), Brahms' Lullaby, Humperdinck's "Children's Prayer" from *Hansel and Gretel.* Also excellent are Mozart's "Concerto for Flute and Harp," "Violin Concerto No. 5 in A major," and "Sinfonia Concertante." One of my personal favorites is Vivaldi's "The Four Seasons," Flute Concertos and Violin Concertos. This music is also suitable for postpartum mothers and other groups.

Selections for Young Children

Include Anderson's "Typewriter symphony," "Serenata," Ugler's "Holiday," and "Syncopated Clock." Also use Debussy's "Cortege," "Ballet," and "La Petit Suite." Grainger's "Spoon River" and Grofe's "Grand Canyon Suite," "On the Trail," Mississippi Suite," and "Huckleberry Finn," Kodaly's "Hary Janus," "Viennese Musical Clock," and Prokofiev's March from "Peter and the Wolf."

I will let you check out the remainder of the music lists and activities listed in Merritt's book.

APPENDIX K

Exercising Your Way Out of Your Right Brain Comfort Zone

"Wait a minute," you say. "How do I know if I am a right brain processor?" Section G is primarily left brain thinking skills. These are the skills which help you succeed in college, in business, in any structured situation. If you have trouble with sequential, logical presentations, feel uncomfortable with your checkbook, self-distract, love art, crafts, music, empathy, you are probably a right brain thinker. Here's how to exercise your way out of discomfort with left brain thinking:

Do any of the activities listed in section G of this Appendix.

- Work crossword puzzles, math problems and other "school" type of activities.
- Shift your phone to your right ear (controlled by your left brain) for analytic listening.
- Set goals and practice what it takes to reach them.
- Prioritize your day's chores on a list. Use sections E and F in this Appendix.
- Do calisthenics, counting sets out loud.

- Analyze body language, including tone of voice.
- Be on time. Not early or late. Schedule your day.
- Eliminate extraneous ideas—distractions from your main idea—when you speak or write.
- Write out your most frustrating problem in an outline form.
- Practice rational opinions and presentations.

APPENDIX L

Exercise Your Way Out of Your Left Brain Comfort Zone

You know you are either a left brain processor (or possibly a bilateral processor) if you loved school, are successful in business, enjoy math, lists, organizing, setting priorities, checking progress. Activities listed in Sections E, F, and G are easy for you. In order to feel comfortable with 80% of the females out there and 20% of the males, you need to practice the following:

- Make eye contact with others; try to feel their viewpoint.
- Practice being aware of your environment: smells, sounds, colors, emotions, space.
- Try to see the big picture—the whole situation—how each person or thing is related to others. What effects to they have on the whole?
- Take a five breath vacation: close your eyes and with the first breath, see your favorite scene in your mind's eye as you take slow, deep breaths. On the second breath, consider the sounds of this lovely place. Do tree leaves rustle softly? Waves lap, lap slowly on sand? Laughter? On the third

breath, imagine the smells there. On the fourth, feel what it is like both emotionally and in a tactile sense. Is there warmth and sunshine? A cool breeze? Fun with friends? On the fifth breath, bring yourself back to your situation with a prayer: "Lord, calm my spirit."

- Look for patterns, connections.
- Respond to body language, hug someone, laugh freely, smile, listen to irrelevancies with love. Remember them and reflect them back to the speaker.
- Use positive, supportive self talk.
- Try playing like or with a child, using colorful, childlike language.
- Move, sing, hum, joke, laugh, breath deeply, take a stroll to no place special.
- Shift the phone to your left ear (controlled by your right brain) for empathic listening.

APPENDIX M

How *Stress-free Discipline* Looks in Practice (rarely glitch-free)

See if you can spot the discipline error in the following scenario:

This is a play with four actors: Susan (age 10), Mom, Mike (age 6) and Narrator.

Narrator: Like most mothers, the Mom in our skit needs help. Whenever the action freezes, that's when you, the audience, will help Mom breathe deeply. Why deep breathing? It is the only way to stop the rush of adrenalin that puts us into fight or flight mode. The adrenalin stops our forebrain thinking (where all our acquired skills are) for twenty-three minutes until it wears off. By then another confrontation may set off another rush of adrenalin, perhaps until bedtime. We lose our learned skills. We short circuit our neocortex, which is the center for intellectual and abstract mental activity. We cannot use this part of the brain when we are in "the A-Zone."

High blood pressure, tension in the neck, shoulders, abdomen, indigestion, anxiety, guilt, and insomnia are some of the results of frequent stress hormones—

adrenalin—coursing through your body. Eighty percent of the women in this world are stressed out by confrontations, when adrenalin puts them into the primitive brain stem.

Women have two more ways they react to stress: They seek to nurture children and to connect with other women. Imagine that! When her children are stressing her out, she tries to nurture them. She forgets the rules and lets slide the consequences when she sees that her poor children are stressed by her discipline! She becomes inconsistent in her discipline, thus causing her children to push her more and more in order to get more privileges and exceptions to the rules. While 20% of the men are pushovers, women are the worst offenders. When the children push and the parent gives—too many warnings, not enough tickets—chaos results and much more stress for everyone.

Habitual stress reactions wear out the body, weaken the immune system, sap our strength and pave the way for chronic and sometimes very serious illnesses. Mom, as soon as the whites of your eyes show, your child has control.

So remember, deep breathing is your number one defense against stress—and the first thing you forget when you're under stress. Deep breathing is belly breathing. Shoulder breathing does not renew the oxygen in your blood and brain like belly breathing does (from the diaphragm). Now practice: Breathe in through your nose, pushing out your belly, 2, 3, 4, 5, hold, out, 2, 3, 4, 5, 6, let the air all the way out through your mouth. Relax your shoulders. Do it again. Breathe in by pushing out your belly, 2, 3, 4, 5, hold, out, 2, 3, 4, 5, 6, let the air all the way out. Relax your shoulders. Now you are ready for the play.

Susan: (speaking fast and urgently) "MOM! I get four points each for taking out the trash, brushing my teeth after breakfast and lunch, and putting my jacket and basketball away. That's 20 points. But Mike just held my purse under the sink and ran water in it. He needs mega points taken away under Impulse Control—not just five. What he did is big, Mom. He has to be taught a lesson." (ACTION FREEZES. Mom's shoulders are up around her neck, the whites of her eyes are showing, she's leaning toward Susan with her head forward.)

Narrator: Everybody out there help Mom breathe right. Breathe in by pushing out your belly, 2, 3, 4, 5, hold, out, 2, 3, 4, 5, 6, let the air all the way out. Relax your shoulders. Again. Breathe in by pushing out your belly, 2, 3, 4, 5, hold, out, 2, 3, 4, 5, 6, let the air all the way out. Relax your shoulders.

Mom: (letting out her breath slowly, getting focused on making tic marks—crossing each four with a fifth one to aid counting them up—on her clipboard): "Hmmm, yes. Twenty positive points. Bummer about the purse! Mike gets four points off under...ummm...Impulse Control. What did you do then? Did you smack him? (Susan shakes her head.) O.K., since you controlled your impulse to smack him, that's plus eight points. Then you got to bed on time last night and ate breakfast on time, you get eight positive points. Your total credit so far is—what is it?"

Susan: "Uh...uh... (counting on fingers) thirty-six points. Mom! This is really big!"

Mom: (Speaks slowly, shoulders move down as she breathes, then she gets focused on points) "Right, thirty-six total credit so far today. We'll do debits in a minute. Take some time off and send Mike here, please." (Susan has been looking over Mom's shoulder to make sure she gets all the points she has earned. ACTION STOPS.)

Narrator: When Mom changes her focus from the conflict to the *Stress-free Discipline* process, she avoids the adrenalin rush, the high blood pressure, brain-stem-fight-or-flight thinking, thoughtless discipline and other stress-related problems. She changes her brain chemistry to produce neurotransmitters that promote a sense of well-being, while still keeping pressure on the children to obey rules. When Mom stays on task...giving points...she remains in left brain thinking mode, avoiding the right brain thinking, that is emotions, which would otherwise be triggered by the children's barrage. Because Susan is refocused, she is also calming down, whether she wants to or not. (ACTION STARTS AGAIN)

Mike: (age 6, URGENT, VOICE RAISED) "MOM! Susan broke my remote control truck by kicking it under the bed. She needs points off. This is big, Mom. Don't just take off 4 points on her chart."[108] (ACTION FREEZES)

Narrator: "Everybody out there help Mom breathe right. Breathe in by pushing out your belly, 2, 3, 4, 5, hold, out, 2, 3, 4, 5, 6, let the air all the way out. Relax your shoulders. Again. Breathe in by pushing out your belly, 2, 3, 4, 5, hold, out, 2, 3, 4, 5, 6, let the air all the way out. Relax your shoulders. Stretch." (ACTION STARTS AGAIN)

Mom: (after a breathing, stretching pause) "Sorry about your truck! Susan gets five points off under Impulse Control."

Mike: (SHOUTING AND STAMPING HIS FOOT) "Mom, it's worth at least 10 points off." (ACTION FREEZES)

Narrator: "Everybody out there help Mom breathe right. Breathe in by pushing out your belly, 2, 3, 4, 5, hold, out, 2, 3, 4, 5, 6, let the air all the way out. Relax your shoulders. Again. Breathe in by pushing out your belly, 2, 3, 4, 5, hold, out, 2, 3, 4, 5, 6, let the air all the way out. Relax your shoulders. Mom has been taking two deep breaths and thinking, "How many points did I say? That's what it is." (ACTION STARTS AGAIN)

Mom: "No debate. You must still be mad. What did you do when she kicked your truck?"

Mike: (His lip stuck out) "I held her purse under the sink."

Narrator: "Bear in mind that a smart Mike has already figured out that five points won't satisfy his need for revenge, and that's why he held her purse under the sink. He figures the penalty for his offense is worth the price of seeing Susan's purse awash. Therefore, Mom needs to watch out that she holds him accountable for every infringement of every rule. She also needs to catch Mike being good."

Mom: "Revenge is an impulse control problem. It doesn't fix the broken toy or make your sister stay away from your things. That's why I'm taking five points off on Impulse

Control. The Bible makes sense on these things. "Vengeance is mine, says the Lord" (Romans 12:19).

Mike: (Dejected, squirming, mumbles) "...didn't want a sermon."

Mom: (Ignoring whatever he says there) "By the way, where was your toy when she kicked it?"

Mike: (Moves into Mom's face as he speaks) "In the hallway. MOM! IT'S NOT FAIR. SHE BROKE IT ON PURPOSE." (ACTION FREEZES)

Narrator: "Everybody out there help Mom breathe right. Breathe in by pushing out your belly, 2, 3, 4, 5, hold, out, 2, 3, 4, 5, 6, let the air all the way out. Relax your shoulders. Again. Breathe in by pushing out your belly, 2, 3, 4, 5, hold, out, 2, 3, 4, 5, 6, let the air all the way out. Relax your shoulders. Stretch." (ACTION STARTS AGAIN)

Mom: (breathing deeply, no smiles or debate, letting silence fall, shoulders again relaxing) "What kind of rule do we have that prevents this breakage of your toys? If your toys stayed put away when you're not actively playing, would that solve the problem?"

Mike: "Uh, yeah, I guess. I left it out."

Mom: "Minus four on making a mess and you didn't take your plate to the sink after you ate breakfast. Minus another four. You spilled milk on the table and I had to clean up after you. Minus another four. Did you clean up something without being told today?"

Mike: (Getting pushy) "Yeah, Mom, I brushed my teeth after breakfast. You hafta give me points for that! Let me see what you have." (He grabs for the clipboard, but cannot get it away from Mom. ACTION FREEZES)

Narrator: "Mike is striding center stage in an effort to take control. Mom must be strong. Everybody out there help Mom breathe right. Breathe in by pushing out your belly, 2, 3, 4, 5, hold, out, 2, 3, 4, 5, 6, let the air all the way out. Relax your shoulders. Again. Breathe in by pushing out your belly, 2, 3, 4, 5, hold, out, 2, 3, 4, 5, 6, let the air all the way out. Relax your shoulders. Stretch." (ACTION STARTS AGAIN)

Mom: (Again silence while Mom breathes, no smiles, no frowns. She is quietly calm, eyebrows slightly raised) "Funny, I checked your toothbrush after breakfast and it wasn't used. From now on, you'll have to brush your teeth in the kitchen so I can see you do it. That's five points off for lying, also five points off for impulse control problem, grabbing and disrespect."

Susan: (eavesdropping) "Mike's lying about the truck, too, Mom. I didn't break his toy, it was already broken."

Mom: "Susan, go to your room."

Susan: (Getting red in the face) "No Mom, it's not fair! When are you going to really punish him? He gets away with everything." (ACTION FREEZES)

Narrator: "Here we go! Everybody out there help Mom breathe right. Breathe in by pushing out your belly, 2, 3, 4, 5, hold, out, 2, 3, 4, 5, 6, let the air all the way out. Relax your shoulders. Again. Breathe in by pushing out your belly, 2, 3, 4, 5, hold, out, 2, 3, 4, 5, 6, let the air all the way out. Relax your shoulders. Stretch. Mom has to use the 'I mean it' look: no smiles, no frown, easy posture, shoulders down, no talk." (ACTION STARTS AGAIN)

Mom: (When Susan's gone) "What happened, Mike?"

Mike: "She broke it more when she kicked it. I could play with it before the wheels fell all the way off."

Narrator: "Mom has no way of knowing what really happened. She chooses to neutralize the negativity before continuing with points. She's not going to put herself in the umpire position."

Mom: (Shoulders down and back, no smiles or frowns) "Both of you children sit at the kitchen table and say three specific things the other person did right today. (She starts writing down points as specifics come to light that aren't already on the chart.)

Both children, sitting:
"Aw, Mom..." (Silence falls. Children squirm and mutter complaints. More silence).

Narrator: "Prayer for forgiveness at this point is a real bonus for all concerned. "[109]

Mom: (no smiles or frowns, she waits, praying)

Mike: "OK. Susan was nice to me this morning."

Mom: "No, that's not specific. Try again."

Mike: "Uh, she emptied her trash. Uh…she cleaned up water on the bathroom floor."

Susan: "Yeah, OK. Mike got up by himself on time." (Mom is writing down points as specifics come to light that aren't already on the chart.) "Um, he emptied his trash basket and hung up his pajamas."

Narrator: "Notice that Mom doesn't have to be everywhere at all times to catch her children being good. The children do it for her"

Mom: "Let's pray. 'Father God, Lord Jesus, please forgive us as we forgive others. Help us to forgive. We're giving up our anger and our demand for punishment to you. Please replace our mean feelings with your grace. Amen.'"

Narrator: "By the time only positive points are listed, the children's' anger will probably dissipate. However, negative points for breakage should be accompanied with reasonable natural consequences."

Mom: "Susan, I want you to try to fix the truck. If you can't fix it, give it to Dad when he comes home. Also, you need to apologize for kicking it."

Susan: "I'm sorry."

Mike: "OK."

Mom: "Mike, get a towel and dry everything in Susan's purse, including the bottom of the purse. Then bring it here for me to see."

The End

Did you find the glitch? Mom told the children to say three specific good things about the other child, but let Mike off with only two specifics. These things will happen, since we're human. If you become aware of an error, you may ask your children's forgiveness for your lapse in leadership. If one of your children is helping you hone your discipline skills, he might point it out to you on your Parents' chart. In any case, we do our best and God does the rest!

Natural consequences: Mom needs to award positive points for cleaning up and fixing things. If the truck cannot be fixed, Susan needs to pay for a new one. That's a natural consequence for impulsive behavior.

Then Mom asks for ideas on how to deal with angry feelings and broken toys: What kind of rules might help us deal with broken toys? Children might come up with acceptance of slight breakage, or a "gentle play" rule under impulse problems, or anything that might solve the problem. If the children are on Chart 1 or 2, and lying is a big issue, parents may add it early to Chart 1 or Chart 2.

Just kidding? Not likely: Occasionally a child will claim, "I was just kidding," when in fact he was lying. Lying is intentional deception and it is a hostile act. Take points off for harsh "kidding" under Impulse Control.

In this case, Mom has decided to use individual charts for each child, to track behavior of each one separately. She could have decided to monitor both children together. In that case, negatives might not be brought to her, since she would be subtracting negative points from the reward both children would get. This is a nice way to encourage the children to work out their disagreements together, rather than ruffle Mom with the role of umpire. The choice is up to you.

"How can I be that smart?" you may fairly ask at this point. "I'm not a trained teacher." The answer is, "Either your children are training you or you're training your children." But do not worry. The only thing you need to be a successful parent is to be one step ahead of your children![110]

This system allows you to get ahead of the game they're playing. It allows you time to think, because the point system puts "the ball in their court" more often than it is in yours! The performance burden is off of you and on them. You do not have to invent appropriate non-violent consequences for their misbehavior. You're only the coach, teaching the rules and helping the players do the game of life right.

APPENDIX N

Printable Charts

Children's Point Chart 1

– Negative Points		+ Positive Points	
Making A Mess (Spilling without wiping up, unmade bed, or leaving clothing, toys, etc. around while starting something else)	- 1 each___	**Cleaning Up** (Taking out trash, brushing teeth, carrying plates to sink, putting things away, helping others work.)	+2 each ___
Impulse Control Problem (Example: hitting, grabbing, insults, backtalk)	-2 each___	**Impulse Control and/or Teamwork** (Following directions or "I felt like ___, but instead I did this ___ for our benefit")	+3 each ___
Poor Breakfast or Late Breakfast, or Late Bedtime	- 1 each___	**Healthy Breakfast** On Time and/or In Bed On Time.	+2 each ___
Note: Outright Rebellion gets double consequences 1) Immediate down time or spanking and 2) Points off on the chart	-2 each specific instance	Always start out with positive points – these are Grace Points	Grace Points +10
Negative Points Total	________	Positive Points Total minus Negative Points Total **Total Reward Points**	________ – ________ +/– ________

Parents' Point Chart 1

– Negative Points		+ Positive Points	
Ignoring Chores (1-2 essential chores)	- 1 each	**Performance of an Essential Chore** (giving 5-8 servings of fruits and vegetables to family daily, daily devotional)	+2 each
Impulse Control Problem or Lapse of Leadership (Example: hitting, grabbing, insults, sarcasm, "whatever" attitude)	-2 each	**Impulse Control and/or Leadership** (Following a plan or "I felt like ___, but instead I did this ____ for our benefit")	+3 each
Poor Breakfast or Late Breakfast, or Late Bedtime	- 1 each	**Healthy Breakfast On Time and/or In Bed On Time**	+2 each
		Always start out with positive points – these are Grace Points	Grace Points +10
Negative Points Total	_____	Positive Points Total minus Negative Points Total **Total Reward Points**	________ – ________ +/–_____

Children's Point Chart 2

– Negative Points		+ Positive Points	
Making A Mess (Spilling without wiping up, unmade bed, or leaving clothing, toys, etc., around while starting something else)	- 1 each	**Cleaning Up** (Taking out trash, brushing teeth, carrying plates to sink, putting things away, helping others work.)	+2 each
Impulse Control Problem (Example: hitting, grabbing, insults, backtalk)	-2 each	**Impulse Control and/or Teamwork** (Following directions or "I felt like ___, but instead I did this ___ for our benefit")	+3 each
Poor Breakfast or Late Breakfast, or Late Bedtime	- 1 each	**Healthy Breakfast** On Time and/or In Bed On Time.	+2 each
Any Lie	- 1 each	**Truth Telling** (when it hurts and is to your disadvantage)	+2 each
Note: Outright Rebellion gets double consequences 1) Immediate down time or spanking and 2) Points off on the chart	-2 each specific instance	Always start out with positive points – these are Grace Points	Grace Points +10
Negative Points Total	______	Positive Points Total	________
		minus	–
		Negative Points Total	________
		Total Reward Points	+/– _____

Parents' Point Chart 2

– Negative Points		+ Positive Points	
Ignoring Chores or Making A Mess (Including breakfast and sleep schedule, spilling without wiping up, unmade bed, litter, unfinished work, etc.)	- 1 each	**Cleaning Up or Doing Chores Without Being Told** (Now includes breakfast and sleep on schedule, taking out trash, brushing teeth, carrying plates to sink, putting things away, helping others work.)	+2 each
Impulse Control Problem (Example: hitting, grabbing, insults, backtalk, unnecessary anger)	-2 each	**Impulse Control and/or Teamwork** ("I felt like ___, but instead I did this ____ for our benefit", healthy anger management/ problem solving)	+3 each
Any Lie	- 1 each	**Truth Telling** (When it hurts and is to your disadvantage)	+2 each
Coercion (I win, you lose; using force or threats)	- 1 each	**Win-win Negotiation** (Let's plan to do ___, taking turns, etc.)	+2 each
Note: Outright Rebellion gets double consequences 1) Immediate down time or spanking and 2) Points off on the chart	-2 each specific instance	Always start out with positive points – these are Grace Points	Grace Points +10
Negative Points Total	______	Positive Points Total minus Negative Points Total **Total Reward Points**	________ – ________ +/–_____

Children's Point Chart 3

– Negative Points		+ Positive Points	
Ignoring Chores or Making A Mess (Including breakfast and sleep schedule, spilling without wiping up, unmade bed, litter, unfinished work, etc.)	- 1 each	**Cleaning Up or Doing Chores Without Being Told** (Now includes breakfast and sleep on schedule, taking out trash, brushing teeth, carrying plates to sink, putting things away, helping others work.)	+2 each
Impulse Control Problem (Example: hitting, grabbing, insults, backtalk, unnecessary anger)	-2 each	**Impulse Control and/or Teamwork** ("I felt like ___, but instead I did this ____ for our benefit", healthy anger management/ problem solving)	+3 each
Any Lie	- 1 each	**Truth Telling** (When it hurts and is to your disadvantage)	+2 each
Coercion (I win, you lose; using force or threats)	- 1 each	**Win-win Negotiation** (Let's plan to do ___, taking turns, etc.)	+2 each
Note: Outright Rebellion gets double consequences 1) Immediate down time or spanking and 2) Points off on the chart	-2 each specific instance	Always start out with positive points – these are Grace Points	Grace Points +10
Negative Points Total	_____	Positive Points Total minus Negative Points Total **Total Reward Points**	_______ – _______ +/–_____

Parents' Point Chart

– Negative Points		+ Positive Points	
Ignoring Chores or Making A Mess (2-3 essential chores, poor or late breakfast or bedtime)	- 1 each	**Performance of an Essential Chore or Learn a Good Habit** (Complete breakfast and bedtime on schedule, giving 5-8 servings of fruits and vegetables to family daily, daily devotional, family sports/exercise.)	+2 each
IImpulse Control Problem or Lapse of Leadership (Example: hitting, grabbing, insults, sarcasm, "whatever" attitude)	-2 each	**Impulse Control and/or Leadership** (Following a plan or "I felt like ___, but instead I did this ____ for our benefit")	+3 each
Softie Love (Avoiding confrontations for moral problems, allowing inappropriate selfish behavior.)	- 1 each	**Truth in Love** (Confronting and/or stopping selfish, sinful behavior with growth in view.)	+2 each
		Always start out with positive points – these are Grace Points	Grace Points +10
Negative Points Total	______	Positive Points Total minus Negative Points Total **Total Reward Points**	________ – ________ +/–_____

Youth Point Chart 4

– Negative Points		+ Positive Points	
Ignoring Chores or Making A Mess (Includes breakfast and sleep schedule, spilling without wiping up, unmade bed, litter, unfinished work)	- 1 each	**Cleaning Up or Doing Chores Without Being Told** (Includes breakfast and sleep on schedule, washing dishes, putting things away, helping others work)	+2 each
Impulse Control Problem (Ignoring essential chores, unnecessary anger)	-2 each	**Impulse Control and/or Teamwork** ("I felt like ___, but instead I did this ____ for our benefit", healthy anger management/problem solving)	+3 each
Softie Love (Not confronting moral situations with unpleasant truth, or lying to escape a moral dilemma)	- 1 each	**Truth in love** (Telling the truth when it hurts – particularly when it is to your disadvantage)	+2 each
Coercion (I win, you lose; using force or threats)	- 1 each	**Win-win Negotiation** (Let's plan to do ___, taking turns, etc.)	+2 each
Note: Outright Rebellion gets double consequences 1) Immediate down time or spanking and 2) Points off on the chart	-2 each specific instance	**Swift Obedience** (obedience within 3 seconds)	+2 each
Time-out (lost time for disobedience, Ping Time)	(-1 point per lost minute)	**Bonus Points** (given for maintaining a positive total yesterday)	+2 points

(continued next page)

Youth Point Chart 4, continued

– Negative Points		+ Positive Points	
		Always start out with positive points – these are Grace Points	Grace Points +10
Negative Points Total	_____	Positive PointsTotal minus Negative Points Total **Total Reward Points**	_______ – _______ +/–_____

Parents' Point Chart 4

– Negative Points		+ Positive Points	
Ignoring Chores or Making A Mess (2-3 essential chores, poor or late breakfast or bedtime)	-1 each	**Performance of an Essential Chore or Learn a Good Habit** (Complete breakfast and bedtime on schedule, giving 5-8 servings of fruits and vegetables to family daily, daily devotional, family sports/exercise.)	+2 each
IImpulse Control Problem or Lapse of Leadership (Lack of planning, ignoring essential chores)	-2 each	**Impulse Control and/or Leadership** (Following a plan or "I felt like ___, but instead I did this ____ for our benefit")	+3 each
Softie Love (Avoiding confrontations for moral problems, allowing inappropriate selfish behavior.)	-1 each	**Truth in Love** (Confronting and/or stopping selfish, sinful behavior with growth in view.)	+2 each
Ultimatum (Use of force or threats outside the necessary discipline for unsafe or rebellious behavior.)	-1 each	**Win-win Negotiation or Supportive Solution** (creative problem solving or mediation)	+2 each
		Always start out with positive points – these are Grace Points	Grace Points +10
Negative Points Total	______	Positive Points Total minus Negative Points Total **Total Reward Points**	______ – ______ +/–_____

Youth Point Chart 5

– Negative Points		+ Positive Points	
Ignoring Chores or Making A Mess (Including breakfast and sleep schedule, spilling without wiping up, unmade bed, litter, unfinished work, etc.)	- 1 each	**Cleaning Up or Doing Chores Without Being Told** (Includes breakfast and sleep on schedule, taking out trash, brushing teeth, carrying plates to sink, putting things away, helping others work.)	+2 each
Impulse Control Problem (ignoring essential chores, unnecessary anger)	-2 each	**Impulse Control and/or Teamwork** ("I felt like ___, but instead I did this ____ for our benefit", healthy anger management/ problem solving)	+3 each
Softie Love (Not confronting moral situations with unpleasant truth, or lying to escape a moral dilemma.)	- 1 each	**Truth in Love** (Telling the truth when it hurts – particularly when it is to your disadvantage.)	+2 each
Coercion (I win, you lose; using force or threats)	- 1 each	**Win-win Negotiation** (Let's plan to do ___, taking turns, etc.)	+2 each
Note: Outright Rebellion gets double consequences 1) Immediate down time or spanking and 2) Points off on the chart	-2 each specific instance	**Swift Obedience** (obedience within 3 seconds)	+2 each

(continued next page)

Youth Point Chart 5, continued

– Negative Points		+ Positive Points	
Note: Outright Rebellion gets double consequences 1) Immediate down time or spanking and 2) Points off on the chart	-2 each specific instance	**Win-win Negotiation** (Let's plan to do ___, taking turns, etc.)	+ 2 points
Time-out (lost time for disobedience, Ping Time)	(1 point per lost minute)	**Bonus Points** (given for maintaining a positive total yesterday)	+2 each
Bad Attitude Attack	-2 each	**Fun** – good humor event	+2 each
		Always start out with positive points – these are Grace Points	Grace Points +10
Negative Points Total	_____	Positive Points Total minus Negative Points Total **Total Reward Points**	_______ – _______ +/–_____

Parents' Point Chart 5

– Negative Points		+ Positive Points	
Ignoring Chores or Bad Habit (2-3 essential chores, poor or late breakfast or bedtime)	- 1 each	**Performance of an Essential Chore or Learning a Good Habit** (Complete breakfast and bedtime on schedule, give 5-8 servings of fruits and vegetables to family daily, daily devotional, family sports/exercise.)	+2 each
Impulse Control Problem, or Lapse of Leadership (Lack of planning, ignoring essential chores.)	-2 each	**Impulse Control and/or Leadership** (Using a plan or "I felt like __, but instead I did this __ for our benefit.")	+3 each
Softie Love (Avoiding confrontation of moral problems, allowing inappropriate selfish behavior.)	- 1 each	**Truth in Love** (Confronting and/or stopping selfish, sinful behavior with growth in view.)	+2 each
Ultimatum (Use of force or threats outside the necessary discipline for unsafe or rebellious behavior)	- 1 each	**Win-win Negotia-tion or Supportive Solution** (creative problem solv-ing or mediation)	+2 each
Out of Balance, Bad Attitude Attack (Lack of mental, spiritual, social, physical growth and balance: hardening of the attitudes.)	- 1 each	**Fun-good Humor Events, Positive Balance** (Dynamic growth and balance of mental, spiri-tual, social, physical activities.)	+ 2 each
		Always start out with positive points – these are Grace Points	Grace Points +10

(continued next page)

Parents' Point Chart 5, continued

– Negative Points		+ Positive Points	
Negative Points Total	______	Positive Points Total minus Negative Points Total **Total Reward Points**	______ – ______ +/–______

About the Author

Stress-free Discipline is a system Judith has synthesized using lessons she learned through research, 19 years of teaching (ages 6 through 60) and parenting experience with two gifted sons. Judith graduated from U.C. Berkeley in the 60's with a degree in English and Social Studies.

Early teaching experience in a Stanford University-based high school gave her a head start on educational techniques. Seven years of teaching "at risk" teenagers taught her coping skills which avoid painful parenting. Judith's discipline resources were enriched by experience with violent and emotionally-disturbed youth.

During seven years of teaching high school delinquents, Judith was constantly researching, experiencing what worked and what failed in parenting.

Judith has earned secondary teaching credentials in English and Social Studies in three states, and a California Junior College Life Credential in Banking and Finance. Sixty-four semester units beyond her Bachelor's Degree were devoted to gaining practical skills related to her various teaching assignments. Master's Degree work has focused on Adult Education.

As English Department Chair, Judith wrote culturally relevant instructional materials for the Navajos she taught in Shiprock, New Mexico. She also wrote their four-year high school scope and sequence of computer English curricula. These experiences helped her to build phase-based skills into *Stress-free Discipline.*

Judith was raised a Unitarian, but also explored Buddhism, hypnosis, automatic writing, Transcendental Meditation and Christian Science before committing herself to Christian beliefs. Her faith has been enriched through the hardship of eight years of complete disability caused by Lyme disease, CFIDS, EBV and fibromyalgia. After six years of down time, she wrote this, her "life's work."

She has raised two gifted sons (one hyperactive) as Christians. Now she enjoys her grandchildren, her gardening and Photoshop hobbies. Now Christ-centered family teams are her mission and training parents and children to become Bereans is her goal. She currently resides in Imperial Beach, California with her husband Vicar Michael J. Bonner of St. James Lutheran Church.

End Notes

1 There are exercises to change your thinking patterns in the Appendix.

2 John 14:27.

3 See 1 John 2:16.

4 Like those suffering from genetically or biochemically based ADHD or bipolar

5 Shifting your focus from the discipline battle to this methodology eliminates stress static, changes blood chemistry, lowers blood pressure and clears your mind so answers to tough questions emerge. For details, see Dr. Herbert Benson's book, 🕮 *The Breakout Principle.*

6 Shifting your focus from the discipline battle to this methodology eliminates stress static, changes blood chemistry, lowers blood pressure and clears your mind so answers to tough questions emerge. For details, see Dr. Herbert Benson's book, The Breakout Principle.

7 When the battle is on, the child cannot think well either.

8 Oct. 03, v. 5, p. 485 (10).

9 According to a nationwide online survey conducted by the National Women's Health Resource Center, 30% of Americans feel that sleepiness and fatigue stop them from being productive at work and/or at home.

10 John H. Richardson, quoting Dr. Ed Diener, of the University of Illinois. Interviewed in November, 2002 Reader's Digest.

11 Ephesians 6:4: "Do not provoke your children to wrath by injustice, loss of temper, undue severity, cruelty, favoritism, suppression, sarcasm, ridicule, and misuse or abuse of authority."

Ephesians 6:1-3: "Children, obey your parents in the Lord, for this is right. Honor your father and mother, which is the first commandment with a promise, that it may be well with you, and you may live long on the earth."

12 Proverbs 22:6: "Train up a child in the way he should go, and when he is old he will not depart from it."

13 Proverbs 13:24, Proverbs 22:15, Proverbs 23:13,14.

14 Josh McDowell, *Focus on the Family Magazine,* June/July 2003.

15 "Where Are the Parents?" September 1990, p. 55.

16 See, for example, Philip Greven's book 🕮 *Spare the Child: The Religious Roots of Punishment and the Psychological Impact of Physical Abuse*, Alfred A. Knopf, Inc., 1990.

17 School violence and false self-esteem are linked in an April 2001, *Scientific American* study.

18 Josh McDowell, Op. cit, in relation to parental focus on positive interaction with teens.

19 Conscientiousness, beginning in childhood, is associated with longer life. Researchers at the University of California at Riverside defined this trait as self-discipline, dependability, prudence, care and the will to achieve. According to the UC Berkeley Wellness Letter, February 2004, "These traits may be more important to health over a lifetime than optimism. Or they may be part of it. Thinking carefully before you act—a component of conscientiousness—is not the same thing as optimism. But conscientiousness may provide a sound and realistic underpinning for optimism."

20 It's part of their job description to attempt to get what they want immediately, and they will make your life difficult when they can't have their way. Parents, do not give in. See 1 Samuel 15:22-23, Proverbs 22:6, Proverbs 20:11.

21 For convenience, I'll use either he or she to refer to both sexes in this text.

22 Ecclesiastes 3:13, 2:24-26.

23 A course based on 🕮 *The Seven Habits of Highly Effective People* is offered through FranklinCovey and at many corporations and government agencies such as the United States Department of Homeland Security's Federal Law Enforcement Training Center.

24 This includes high blood pressure, gastrointestinal problems—acid stomach, ulcers, dental problems (teeth grinding), adrenal exhaustion, endocrine imbalances, muscular tension, headache, and often substance abuse.

25 Highly recommended for teachers and parents: Fredric H. Jones and Associates, Inc., 103 Quarry Lane, Santa Cruz, CA 95060. (831) 425-8222. www.fredjones.com. Dr. Jones' textbooks are well worth the time and effort to absorb and practice their contents. Your only regret will be that you did not know about these resources sooner.

26 See www.family.org Heritage Builders section.

27 www.psych.uiuc.edu/~ediener/research/research.html Dr. Ed. Diener of the University of Illinois.

28 John H. Richardson, quoting Dr. Ed. Diener of the University of Illinois, in an interview in the November 2002 Reader's Digest.

29 http://en.wikipedia.org/wiki/Getting_to_YES. An outline of this book can be found at http://www.cozy.org/yes.html.

30 Rachael D. Ramer, *Christian Research Journal*, Volume 26, Number 1, pp. 33-41.

31 Matthew 19:18-24.

32 2 Timothy 1:7. God has not given us the spirit of fear but of love, power and a sound mind.

33 Adult relationships also are destroyed when core fears are not recognized and addressed. See Gary Smalley's book, 🕮 *The DNA of Relationships*, Tyndale House Publishers, Wheaton, IL. www.smalleyonline.com.

34 See www.persecution.com for a real eye-opener.

35 See also a clarification and definition at applest.com/strongwilled.asp. This website contains a self test which is very revealing. Cynthia Tobias has written an excellent book: 🕮 *You Can't Make Me (But I Can Be Persuaded).*

36 See 🕮 *Tools for Teaching* by Dr. Fredric H. Jones, Ph.D with Patrick Jones and JoLynne Jones, Section 1, p. 6, available at www.fredjones.com. Also email info@fredjones.com.

37 These will be items you are asking your child to help you with. Pick one item the first month, two when children graduate to their next chart, etc.

38 If you're afraid of making a child grow up too fast, consider that bonding and realistic self-esteem are established during these years and require some interdependence. False self-esteem is destructive.

39 Partner Learning has been condensed from Chapter 8 of 🕮 *Tools for Teaching* by Dr. Fredric H. Jones, Ph.D. with Patrick Jones and Julienne Jones, Section 1, p. 6, available at www.fredjones.com. Also email info@fredjones.com.

40 Again, see Gary Smalley's book, 🕮 *The DNA of Relationships.*

41 🕮 *Positive Classroom Discipline*, Jones, Fredric H., McGraw Hill, 1987, p. 67. For current publications, See 🕮 *Tools for Teaching* by Dr. Fredric H. Jones, Ph.D. with Patrick Jones and JoLynne Jones, Section 1, p. 6, available at www.fredjones.com. Also email info@fredjones.com.

42 Jones, Fredric. Op. cit. p. 65.

43 🕮 *The Promise of Sleep*, 1999, William C. Dement, Dell Publishing, Random House, New York.

44 Possible chores for each age level are in the Appendix. They may be used in sequence as the child grows up, and should not be considered "hard and fast" rules, but only suggestions. You may wish to write them on cardboard or laminate them, so they can be hung in a central place as a reminder. Add your own specifics after you have tried mine and become used to the system.

45 See 1 Samuel 15:22-23, Proverbs 22:6, Proverbs 20:11.

46 See "The $25,000 idea" in Appendix F.

47 See 🕮 *Tools for Teaching* by Dr. Fredric H. Jones, Ph.D. with Patrick Jones and JoLynne Jones, Section 6, available at www.fredjones.com. Also email info@fredjones.com.

48 Fredric H. Jones, Chapters 15, 16, 🕮 *Tools for Teaching.*

49 See 🕮 *Tools for Teaching* by Dr. Fredric H. Jones, Ph.D. with Patrick Jones and JoLynne Jones, Section 1, p. 6, available at www.fredjones.com. Also email info@fredjones.com.

50 This is belly breathing. Shoulders stay relaxed. See chapter 16, 🕮 *Tools for Teachers.*

51 Dr. Frederic Jones explains this dynamic in lucid detail in Chapter 17, 🕮 *Tools for Teachers.*

52 Shallow breathing fosters anxiety, depression, and physical stress. Change your breathing habits by swimming, singing or other fun deep breathing practices. These will balance your life in a positive way.

53 Again, Dr. Jones has key information on discipline dynamics of body language.

54 What you do with the disputed item is up to you. I recommend a locked closet with chores required to redeem the toy from lockup. Be creative. My brother once took a disputed electronic game away from his quarreling children while his wife drove the car. He threw it out the window. As it broke to pieces and disappeared from sight, he uttered one simple sentence which the children never forgot: "We don't fight over *things* in this family." Ten lectures could not have achieved the same success.

55 See 🕮 *Tools for Teaching* by Dr. Fredric H. Jones, Ph.D. with Patrick Jones and Jo Lynne Jones, Chapter 18, available at www.fredjones.com. Also email info@fredjones.com.

56 See 🕮 *Tools for Teaching* by Dr. Fredric H. Jones, Ph.D. with Patrick Jones and Jo Lynne Jones, page 184, available at www.fredjones.com. Also email info@fredjones.com.

57 A half-size clipboard for charts is available at Staples for $1.20.

58 Habitual obedience toward parents translates into easy obedience to God as the child matures. Get this right even if it consumes all your free time for months. See 1 Samuel 2:12-17,22-36, 1 Samuel 3:13, 4:12-18.

59 Luke 12:48.

60 Parasites may be airborne, water borne, or communicated by other means. Colon regularity is essential to family health and most often overlooked. Blood or hair can be tested for nutritional deficiencies. Saliva can be pH tested to achieve balance in the oxygen delivery system essential to appropriate thinking and acting. See Appendix on pH testing.

61 "Many live as enemies of the cross of Christ, worshipping the god of our appetites" (Philippians 3:18b-19).

62 2 Corinthians 12:9

63 You can practice prioritizing as part of impulse control. Contact me at www.stressfreediscipline.org for tools if you have trouble with prioritizing.

64 See page 65 for more ideas on teaching impulse control.

65 See pages 35-36 for beginning charts.

66 2 Timothy 1:7.

67 An excellent book to clarify this is 🕮 *Speaking the Truth in Love* by Ruth Koch and Kenneth C. Haugk, published by Stephen Ministries, St. Louis, Missouri.

68 1 John 3:1,2.

69 While Point Chart 3 correlates with the maturity of the average 7 to 10-year-old, some may have problems with the more complex ideas found in Win-win negotiations. Be patient. They'll understand if you explore what's "fair for everyone." Consequences of a choice must be clearly understood.

70 This is a good time for daily point totals.

71 Schoolwork comes under impulse control. Check with teachers weekly to see if the work is getting done and turned in. Deduct points for lost or forgotten assignments.

72 About sports, after school jobs and growth spurts: exhaustion doesn't excuse you from chores, and neither does it excuse your children. Solutions include medical checkups to rule out anemia and other

physical problems, earlier bedtimes, restricted TV, cooking 30 entrees once a month (See 🕮 *Once A Month Cooking*, available from Focus on the Family—www.family.org) and doing most of the chores on Saturday. I only recommend jobs for homeschoolers—then only if they want one.

About sleep: a Harvard sleep study indicates that teens need nine (9) hours of sleep through age 18 in order to be most effective in school.

73 This is a good time for daily point totals.

74 Schoolwork comes under Impulse Control. Check with teachers weekly to see if the work is getting done and turned in. Deduct points for lost or forgotten assignments. Organize stuff into files: English, Math, Science, etc. Put big assignments on family calendar.

75 These are pragmatic definitions based on my purposes for this text. The dictionary will give you a more complete definition.

76 Family morning exercises are recommended: a combination of stretches, calisthenics and aerobics. Daughters may be exempted during "monthly curse" distress, but exercise—along with appropriate minerals and additional sleep—often relieves distress.

77 Remember, schoolwork comes under Impulse Control. Check with teachers weekly to see if the work is getting done and turned in. Deduct points for lost or forgotten assignments.

78 Right and left brain thinking is briefly explained in the Appendix.

79 This is a good pattern for your old age, as they'll be conditioned to helping you when you need it.

80 When you reward hasty or incomplete work, you lower your standard of excellence. Thus, you teach a dysfunctional work ethic and your child cannot compete in the real world as an adult.

81 "The mind cannot focus on the opposite of an idea," according to Dr. Dennis Waitley, a motivational psychologist who has studied and worked with POWs, Super Bowl teams, and others.

82 Help children differentiate between general and specific by modeling it yourself.

83 This is a favorite disobedience ploy. Charm wins many concessions.

84 Keep it within your reach, preferably on your wristwatch. Never put the timer into your child's control.

85 You may have to hold a strong-willed child in a chair for the time-out. Jumping off the chair brings spanking.

86 Impulse control involves thinking of consequences ahead of the event, solving problems before they become crises.

87 At Point Chart 3 you have the option of watching for their skill at negotiating or using the Impulse Control section to record interactions.

88 Since boys and girls, men and women process information differently, it is important that each person learns to think outside his or her comfort zone. Respect for divergent thinking styles is an important value to teach. Thinking like the other person is essential for successful negotiation and living together. However, it takes practice. Encourage your children to include among their friends people who think differently and have different interests. That way, you don't both have the same blind spots, and you force yourselves to grow. Friendship is not about finding a clone, nor is marriage.

89 Cynthia Tobias has written well on this issue in 🕮 *You Can't Make Me Do It (But I Can be Persuaded)*, $18 from www.family.org.

90 *Once a Month Cooking* by Mimi Wilson, available from Barnes and Noble for $11.65.

91 April, 2001 Scientific American, Op. cit.

92 Further, historically, every decrease in respect for others is linked to increased abuse. For example, abortion on demand brings with it higher child abuse rates.

93 Delinquents usually have very poor reading skills. After six years of teaching delinquent teens, I believe their anger is fueled by their lack of coping skills. Life skills, especially reading, are an essential part of a healthy lifestyle.

94 This clipboard is a distancing tool so you'll avoid the trap of emotional responses. You are then free to breathe deeply, observe dispassionately, quell your inflamed pride, and be proactive in solving the problems.

95 You will be fascinated by resources from WallBuilder Press regarding 🕮 *Education and the Founding Father*s and 🕮 *The Bulletproof George Washington*. Write to P.O. Box 397, Aledo, Texas 76008; (817) 441-6044 or see at www.wallbuilders.org.

96 Use this format: Lasting love is a type of what? (behavior, commitment or feeling?) with the following characteristics: it forgives, it takes constant work to maintain, it considers the loved one's needs at least equal to one's own, saying "no" when it needs to be said, setting boundaries and rules of behavior, telling the truth, etc.

97 A problem-solving matrix is provided in the Appendix for your convenience in teaching this skill to your child. Refer to it often.

98 These are college level thinking skills poorly taught—if at all—in classrooms which must teach to the lowest common denominator. See Appendix for a skeletal format with methods to use in teaching these.

99 Remember: the U.C. Riverside researchers identified conscientiousness (thinking carefully before you act) with long life. They said, "it may be more important to health over a lifetime than optimism."

100 The ability to evaluate is the highest thought process and the most difficult.

101 Delinquents usually have very poor reading skills. After six years of teaching delinquent teens, I believe their anger is fueled by their lack of coping skills. Life skills, especially reading, are an essential part of a healthy lifestyle.

102 www.naturalhealthmag.com; *Natural Health*, January/February 2003.

103 Again, Dr. Jones to the rescue! He has many educational games in his repertoire.

104 Your brain needs 40% more oxygen than the rest of your body in order to function well. This is important. You will not only think better, you will also fall prey to fewer infections when you have more oxygen in your blood.

105 See Julie Ann Barnhill's book, 🕮 *She's Gonna Blow* for a detailed discussion of mothers and anger management.

106 You might want to give God's column 32 possible points, so He can "outvote" you. How committed are you to His leadership?

107 🕮 *Mind, Music, and Imagery: Unlocking the Treasures of Your Mind*, Aslan Publishing, Santa Rosa, CA, (707) 542-5400. ISBN 0-944031-62-5.

108 Notice Mike wants to control the situation by negotiation or changing the deal. Don't give in, Mom!

109 Forgiveness comes under Impulse Control. Because it's hard to measure, parents must observe behavior to see if it's still vengeful after the prayer that we be forgiven as we have forgiven others. Points can be awarded after time has passed and there is no sign of leftover resentment.

110 The way to eat an elephant is one bite at a time.